INSTRUCTOR'S MANUAL
GORDON MORK

NINTH EDITION

A HISTORY OF CIVILIZATION

ROBIN W. WINKS

CRANE BRINTON
JOHN B. CHRISTOPHER
ROBERT LEE WOLFF

Prentice Hall, *Upper Saddle River, New Jersey 07458*

© 1996 by PRENTICE-HALL, INC.
Simon & Schuster / A Viacom Company
Upper Saddle River, New Jersey 07458

All rights reserved

10 9 8 7 6 5 4 3 2 1

ISBN 0-13-228347-6

Printed in the United States of America

INTRODUCTION: FOR THE INSTRUCTOR

This manual is based upon more thirty years of college teaching experience, several semesters classroom experience with the seventh and eighth editions of this textbook, and a careful reading of the page proofs of the NINTH EDITION.

All the chapters are set up with parallel structures. I begin with my concept of the MAJOR GOAL of the chapter, a brief description of the changes in the NINTH EDITION, and the BASIC OBJECTIVES which I suggest for the chapter. Then follow some comments on the BOXES, documentary or analytical material which is pregnant with possibilities for discussion. Thus, the first part of each chapter of this manual deals with vital matters: I, for one, think they are items which are so important that they might be seen as the "things every students should know."

The section-by-section portion which follows, on the other hand, deals with material which is important, but often complex (and, to some, obscure). The TO DEFINE AND DISCUSS items could be used for identification quizzes, of course, but I see them rather as items which you need to address in class if you think it is essential that the majority of your students are to get anything out of them beyond rote memorization.

Finally, I comment on the SUMMATION of each chapter and add a note on the CRITICAL THINKING section. This CRITICAL THINKING section is new to this edition of the textbook. A number of serious questions are posed for the students, and for us as instructors as well. If you are using the TEST ITEM FILE, you will see these questions arise again in the essay items there. In short, students can use the CRITICAL THINKING questions to prepare for the essay test, if you wish to use the items that way. Or, they are simply there to inspire some useful discussions in class.

My students often ask me a question like this: "How do I know which of the material, from all that in the textbook, is really important?" I usually answer that the authors have given them significant guidance. Any item named in a chapter heading or subheading is "important." The topics of the BOXES and most of the ILLUSTRATIONS are "important." The concepts described and the persons or events mentioned in the SUMMARY and CRITICAL THINKING sections are "important." The revision of the TEST ITEM FILE for the NINTH EDITION. will keep these criteria in mind. When you find subjects which you believe are of special importance, but which are not strongly emphasized in the textbook (as well you might, because each of us has our own priorities) be sure to stress that point to your class.

The authors of this textbook indicate that the questions which historians ask are more important, ultimately, than any particular set of historical information. The main purpose of education, they imply, is the development of intellectual skills. You might take a look at Robin Winks's videotape on "What some good historians do," available from the Association of Yale Alumni (1-800-236-9253), to get some additional insights on how he approaches history. But, as a former Chairman of the National Endowment for the Humanities has pointed out, emphasis on process without content can result in vast areas of ignorance among presumably educated people. So the content is important, and this book provides it in abundance.

In the final analysis, the best instructor's manual is the textbook itself. Even if you are pressed for time, be sure to review the introductory essays to each chapter, the BOXES, the bibliographical suggestions, the MAPS, the SUMMARIES, and the CRITICAL THINKING questions. I spend one of my first sessions with my class walking the students through the book, so they get a chance to see what it is like and how they can use its various features. They should note, for example, that the INDEX includes a pronunciation guide. You should lead them carefully through the PREFACE (which most will tend to skip), because it gives them vital clues about how to make best use of the book.

As you develop your class using this textbook and INSTRUCTOR'S MANUAL, you may find that you disagree with some of my suggestions, and I take no umbrage at that. I just hope my ideas will set you to thinking about how better to address your classes with the challenges and beauties of the history of our civilization.

A SPECIAL NOTE

To those of you who are not using Volume I (or the Combined Volume) of the textbook: Your students will be starting out in midstream, without the benefit of the background afforded by the first chapters. It is essential that you deal creatively with that situation, because whatever other version you use, you will be starting more or less in the middle of a complex set of developments. Your students, therefore, will lack some important knowledge which they would have had if they were using the complete textbook.

One way to handle this situation is to have them acquire the entire textbook, even if they are not going to be assigned the whole thing. Material from the early chapters can be assigned selectively and/or the early material can be used for reference. If this is not feasible, you might wish to put a copy of volume I on reserve for their occasional use and prepare a lecture or two referring directly to the textbook's chapters which they do not have, to give them a running start. No doubt you will give introductory lectures anyway. Or, you might have them go through the first chapter of their version of the book and prepare a list of "stump the professor" questions, i.e. items which are mentioned in their first chapter but which are not fully explained, because they were dealt with earlier in the book. This will enable you to identify gaps in their knowledge (certainly not in your own) and repair those gaps before going into the content of the first chapter for which they will be fully responsible.

Several years have passed since the previous edition of this textbook was published, and the world has changed a great deal. The dynamics begun in the late 1980's are still with us, and the outcomes which are deriving from the fall of the communist empires and the end of the cold war are not yet fully clear. Perhaps Craine Brinton, one of the original authors of the textbook, is watching the latest developments from some celestial university chair. He might no doubt suggest that we look again at the original version of his book, *Anatomy of Revolution*, which called into question Marxist analysis back in the 1930's and offered other comparative approaches with which to understand historical patterns.

GRM
Lafayette, Indiana
10/95

1. THE FIRST CIVILIZATIONS

The MAJOR GOAL of this chapter is twofold: from the standpoint of information, it is designed to familiarize the students with ancient civilizations, of which almost all of your students will be entirely ignorant; more importantly, from the standpoint of approach, it is designed to give your students a good start on the study of history itself. Most of your students will believe (and/or fear) that studying history means simply memorizing long lists of unfamiliar names and dates. Because of the relative obscurity of most of this early material for them, BEWARE lest their worst fears be realized. Rather, you should emphasize that INQUIRY is the key to mastering history. To be sure, one does have to get a handle on the raw data. But the authors have emphasized the questions that are being raised and the relatively new answers which are coming from recent studies in the archaeology and the languages of this era. As they say, "discoveries continue at a rapid pace." This chapter on the world of long ago, therefore, is very dependent on new knowledge, just as a textbook in aeronautical engineering would be.

To emphasize this point, you may want to urge your students to search current news sources for information on the most recent archeological digs, and bring the articles to class. Within the most recent couple of months of this writing, for example, archeologists have announced the discovery of previously unknown tombs in North Africa and the Middle East.

REVISIONS FOR THE NINTH EDITION: The basic text of this chapter has been trimmed of some of its verbiage and minor details, but its framework and essentials remain unchanged. Five of the BOXES have been eliminated, and two of the remaining ones have been shortened a bit. You should emphasize that when the authors insert a BOX, there is good reason. The BOXES give excellent materials for class discussion.

BASIC OBJECTIVES

1. Each chapter in this book begins with an outline of headings and sub-headings, and the minimal basic objective of each chapter should be that every student should know what the authors mean by the words used in that outline.

old stone age
new stone age
Mesopotamia and Elam
Hittites, Hurrians, Canaanites, Philistines, Phoenicians
Minoans
Mycenae
Homer and the "Dark Age"

2. The student should recognize and be able to identify, define, or locate on a map, the key concepts, persons, places, and events treated in the chapter.

homo sapiens
urban life
hydraulic society
ka
Lascaux
Jericho
Sumer
cuneiform
Gilgamesh
Ebla
Hammurabi
Amenhotep IV (Akhenaten)
Book of the Dead
Indo-Aryan
Semitic
monotheism
Bronze Age
Assyria
Palestine
Ugarit
Old Testament (Hebrew Bible)
King David
Linear A and B
Trojan War
the Iliad and the Odyssey

ITEMS in 1 AND 2 MIGHT BE USEFUL AS IDENTIFICATION QUIZ ITEMS.

3. The students should come to consider just how old humankind is on this earth, and just what kind of argument and evidence has been marshaled to support various theories. In some cases, this may get you into discussions of the origins of species and the authority of the Bible. If you have any students who have studied geology, make use of their knowledge to show how recently (in geologic time) homo sapiens appeared, and how much more recently the written record appeared. The time chart on p. 5 is useful, and you may wish to assign someone to turn it into a proportional time line to dramatize the point.

4. Maps are essential to give the students an idea of where the unfamiliar place names are located, but also in showing the changes over time. If the students have it available, have them compare the MAP on p. 7 with a map of the modern Middle East later in the book. Students may be remarkably naive about maps: when I was a youth, I had the idea that the "holy land" was an entirely mythical place, existing only in scripture. Some of your students might not be better informed. GET THEM USED TO STUDYING THE MAPS.

5. The publishers of this book have gone to much trouble and expense (which ultimately your students must bear) to provide photos of historical places and things, many of them in excellent color. Spend

some time on the pictures in class, lest students skip over them or see them only as attempts to add a design factor to the book. For example, have them compare the Tower of Babel of Breughel with the photo of the ziggurat at Nippur.

BOXES

The BOXES are labelled either "Doing History" or "The Written Record," to distinguish between methodlogical questions and primary sources. Chances are that most students will skip over them when they are reading the book, unless you do something special with them. Here is an excellent chance for discussion! History is not just a list to be memorized, but an approach for inquiry. For example-

BOX p. 8, "place names" [doing history]. Note the importance of the names by which places are called. Who has the right to give the name, and what does the name imply. In this chapter the realtionship is often between ancient local names and the Biblical names of the Judeo-Christian tradition. But the authors also cite a twentieth century example, the shift in Russia from St. Petersburg to Leningrad and back to St. Petersburg.

BOX p. 11, "Gilgamesh." [written record]. Note the relatioship between the Judeo-Christian story and the Sumerian epic.

BOX p. 12, "Hammurabi" [written record]. You might elicit some interesting comments from pre-law students, or from ask for conclusions about the position of women and slaves in that society. This source is shorter than in the eighth edition.

BOX p. 18, "Cursing Litany" [written record]. The poem/incantation has been shortened from the previous edition. It could be used as a class exercise in choral reading, with two halves of the class reading alternative lines.

I. BEFORE WRITING

Because of the importance of the written record for historians, many of us, and our students, will tend to skip over the "prehistory" period as unimportant or as material "lost in the mists of the past." Yet some of our civilization is built both literally and figuratively on the stones of these earlier civilizations. Moreover, the questions of how civilizations develop and how they survive (or not) is vital today.

For students who are caught up in the newest in technology, and might therefore be contemptuous of the study of the deep past, note for them the importance of high tech approaches, such as radiocarbon dating.

TO DEFINE AND DISCUSS: These items will doubtless be entirely unfamiliar to most students, and their mention in the textbook or in lecture will likely be puzzling to them. Thus they are things which need to be discussed and explained by you, if you want your students to understand them and gain some real familiarity with them. In some cases, realistically, you may wish to treat these items as interesting details of secondary importance, as opposed to the really major items listed above under BASIC OBJECTIVES.

Homo habilis and homo erectus
Archbishop Ussher's chronology
Jericho and Catal Hüyük

II. THE VALLEY PEOPLES AND IRAN

Sumerian and Egyptian civilizations are remote to most of our students, but not entirely unknown to them. Either through religious training, though museum visits, or through references to the background of the the contemporary Middle East, the more alert of your students will bring some ideas (or misconceptions) about these things into your classroom.

The 1990/91 war with Iraq brought some interest in the Mesopotamian civilizations. Saddam Husein and the Iraqis, whatever their sins, were able to call upon a heritage of ancient greatness when they wish to do so.

You might start with asking how many of your students have heard of "King Tut." Find him in the textbook [p. 14] and build backward and forward from there. Or you do the same with the Sphinx and the pyramids. Most productive, however, might be a brief discussion of the Rosetta Stone, which shows the importance of language to our understanding of the civilization in question.

TO DEFINE AND DISCUSS:
Akkadian
Babylonian
Assyrian
Nebuchadnezzar
pharaoh
Karnak
Osirus and Isis
hieroglyphics
Queen Nefertiti.

III. PEOPLES OUTSIDE THE VALLEYS
&
IV. CRETE AND MYCENAE

Of all the peoples discussed in this chapter, most of your students will probably have the greatest familiarity with the Hebrews. In this section of the chapter that people is put into its historical context, and important points are made about the Hebrew Bible as a source of historical information.

Cretan civilization, also called Minoan, and Bronze Age Greece, also called Mycenaean civilization, will make more sense to your students if you have them skip ahead to the map in the next chapter. Yet is important that it be introduced contemporaneously with the discussions of the Eastern Mediterranean cultures, to keep the early Greek developments in context.

TO DEFINE AND DISCUSS:

Hysksos
Uriah the Hittite
Sea Peoples
Israel and Judah
Yahweh and Jehovah
Cyrus the Great
Knossos
the Trojan War
various Greek gods and goddesses

SUMMATION

Though some of the links of our own times with the worlds approached in this chapter seem tenuous indeed, others are so clear that they seem to destroy the very concept of time. The challenge of teaching this chapter is to capture your students, who are likely to be very present-minded, and link them to the past. For some of the students the romance of an age long gone, cities long buried, and tongues long forgotten may do the trick. For others a reminder that stories, ideals, and conflicts first established in the ancient Mediterranean world still move men and women to love and to hate, may help them bridge the barrier of time.

CRITICAL THINKING SKILLS

An attractive new feature of the NINTH EDITION is the addition of a section at the end of each chapter adding several questions to encourage each student to grapple with important questions raised by the material in that chapter.
Each of these would be useful for class discussion (if your class is small enough), as rhetorical questions to address in your lecture (for larger sections), for written exercises for your students out of class, for study items before exams, and (in slightly modified forms) as test items.

The TEST ITEM FILE which accompanies this textbook and MANUAL will have suggested test items based upon each of the CRITICAL THINKING questions for that chapter, as well as some questions which call upon students to bridge material and questions from more than one chapter.

Thus, to help students get ready of exams, they might study the CRITICAL THINKING questions.

2. THE GREEKS

The MAJOR GOAL of this chapter is to familiarize the students with the history and culture of what is generally known as the "ancient Greeks," though important portions of the Greek story are told in Chapter 1. Our modern civilization is closely related to that of the Greeks, partly because many of its intrinsic values are not unlike our own, and partly because for many generations virtually all the leaders of our civilization were educated with constant reference to the Greeks. In a sense the very course you are teaching is one of the last vestiges of that tradition.

Changes for the NINTH EDITION: There is some additional material on women, but otherwise few changes in this chapter for the new edition. Some of the details have been deleted and some material has been rewritten for clarification.

BASIC OBJECTIVES

1. Each student should understand and be able to describe, or locate on a MAP, the major items used in the chapter headings.

the Persian Empire
Ionian cities
Marathon
the Athenian Empire
the Peloponnesian Wars
Hellenistic
Sparta
Thebes
philosophy

2. The student should recognize and be able to identify or define the major concepts, things, and persons of the chapter.

Herodotus and Thucydides
Pericles
polis and poleis
helots
Draco and Draconian
Zoroastrianism
Alexander the Great
the Parthenon
Socrates
Plato and Aristotle

3. This chapter deals both with Greek political (and military) history and with the high culture of Greek civilization, first the one and then

the other. You may wish to consider the relationship between these two elements of the story. The comings and goings of various Greek political leaders probably is of little significance to us now, but they did provide the circumstances in which the tremendous creativity of the Greeks flowered. Cleisthenes and Alcibiades are far less important than Plato and Euripides, yet they are treated first in the text. Be sure your students don't get bogged down in the political details and miss the cultural giants.

You may even wish to suggest that Section V, on Greek culture, be read first, and then follow it with Sections I-IV.

4. In common parlance the contrast between Athenian democracy and Spartan militarism is often drawn, and drawn too sharply. This chapter does a good job of pointing out the limitations of the democracy of Athens. It also provides a good opportunity to get the students to reflect on the limits of our own democracy.

5. Students who see little immediate relevance of a study of ancient Greece might be challenged to look around them to see what evidence in their own immediate environment shows the direct influence of Greek ideals of the good, the true, and the beautiful. What state does not have a few towns named after Greek cities? What university campus (or local civic buildings) show no evidence of Greek architectural models? Even the Greek letters used by campus organizations, both social and honorary, remind us of our links with the past.

BOXES

BOX p. 35, "Pericles' Oration" [written record]. Written by (or recorded by) Thucydides, this is a major document of Western Civilization. The idealized concept of freedom and democracy should be appreciated by the students, and then compared critically with the realities of Athenian history as shown in the textbook.

BOX p. 41, "The Olive in Greek Civilization" [a closer look]. This commentary combines mythology (Athena and Poseidon) economic history.

BOX p. 44, "Aristophanes on 'Worthy Themes'" [written word]. This BOX has been expanded, both in introductory comments and in text. Aristophanes' play, "The Frogs," is a comedy, but the passage selected deal with a serious topic. "High thoughts," he says, "must have high language." Try writing that motto on the your syllabus, and see if it gets a rise out of your students. Maybe Aristophanes was using a bit of irony here after all.

Now let us turn to the specific subheadings of the chapter for consideration of several important details.

I. THE GREEKS BEFORE THE PERSIAN WARS

Students tend automatically to think in terms of the national state, so it is important that the concept of the city-state be firmly established, not only to help them understand ancient Greece, but so that they can deal with much of medieval and early modern history as well. Sparta and Athens are shown in this section as models of two ways to organize a polity. In each case, however, the fact that only a few MEN were citizens is made clear.

TO DEFINE AND DISCUSS:
acropolis
agora
Lycyrgus and Solon
barbarian
slavery

II. PERSIA AND THE GREEKS, TO 478 B.C.

The newer editions have introduced better material on the Persians, and one might remind the students that Persia is in the same place (though it is hardly the same country) as modern Iran. The confrontation between the small Greek city-states and the vast Persian Empire is a story which has stirred many a generation.

TO DEFINE, LOCATE, AND DISCUSS: Anatolia
Cyrus and Darius
Xerxes
Athens' navy.
Zarathustra

III. THE ATHENIAN EMPIRE, 478-404 B.C.
&
V. RELIGION, WRITING, AND THOUGHT

Periclean Athens was one of the major cultural high points of our civilization and should be given its due, even though the authors of this book correctly point out some of its injustices and shortcomings. The great clash with Sparta known as the Peloponnesian Wars has provided the introduction to the heroism and terror of war for centuries for the leaders of our civilization. Be sure to link the political and military history of this era with the section V, on cultural developments.

TO DEFINE AND DISCUSS:
alliance vs. empire
the _demos_
Syracuse
Olympian gods
Delphic oracles
the death of Socrates
Plato's *Republic*
Doric, Ionic, and Corinthian columns
Aristotle and the sciences

IV. THE FOURTH CENTURY B.C. AND THE HELLENISTIC AGE

One could spend all semester on the wars and treacheries of the various leaders of the Greek city-states, and once that was a major portion of any introduction to ancient world history. Now some of this detail is quite properly eliminated. But the rise of the man we still know as Alexander the Great is still a major point. Perhaps students will be attracted by the fact that Alexander was so young. Perhaps they will be put off by the emphasis on the ideal of the conquering hero. Perhaps they will see Alexander's HUBRIS as indicative of the ultimate Greek tragedy. In any case, they should be taught that Alexander's political conquests, however temporary, led to the opening of Greek (or Hellenistic) culture to vast areas on the world we now call the Middle East, and that Greek culture dominated much of that area till the fall of Constantinople in 1453 A.D., and even beyond. Spend some time with them on the MAPS, perhaps using TRANSPARENCIES.

TO DEFINE, LOCATE, AND DISCUSS:
Macedonia
King Philip
the Ptolemies
the Seleucids, Ptolemies, and Antigonids
Alexandria

SUMMATION

Whether one starts with geography, politics, war, or the arts, one cannot leave Greece without the serious consideration of the ideals expressed by the philosophers. The very word--the love of learning--is our greatest heritage from the Greeks. The Doctor of Philosophy, a title many of those of you reading this manual have earned, reminds us of the Greeks. To be sure, Socrates would be astounded (and no doubt dismayed) at some of the things that our modern academies have become. But be that as it may, your students should leave this chapter knowing that their education has solid links to the good, the true, and the beautiful as set forth in ancient Greece.

Question: Would our democracy put Socrates to death for corrupting the youth?

CRITICAL THINKING QUESTIONS

Use these for discussion, or for springboards to lecture topics. The essay questions at the end of the TEST ITEM FILE will revisit them is slightly altered form.

3. THE ROMANS

The MAJOR GOAL of this chapter is to familiarize the students with the rise and fall of ancient Rome. Ever since Gibbon wrote in the eighteenth century, the question of why the magnificent Roman Empire fell has been a major point of discussion and debate. In this textbook the chapter on Rome and the next chapter on Judaism and Christianity overlap chronologically, so the question is inevitably treated in both chapters. If your situation permits, you may wish to consider taking chapters 3 and 4 as a single unit rather than treating them separately.

Changes for the NINTH EDITION: The structure of the chapter remains the same as in the eighth edition, though a number of details have been cut to shorten the account. Two of the BOXES and several of the illustrations have been eliminated.

BASIC OBJECTIVES

1. Every student should have a grasp of the major items listed in the chapter headings and subheadings.

the Roman Republic
Caesar
the Triumvirate
the Roman Empire
Augustus
Nero
Marcus Aurelius
Diocletian

2. Students should be able to recognize, identify or locate on a MAP, and describe the major items mentioned in the chapter.

patricians and plebeians
SPQR
Etruscans
the Twelve Tables
the Punic Wars
Marius
Sulla
Pompey
Marc Anthony
Pax Romana
Praetorian Guard
Trojan
Cicero
Vergil

Tacitus
Galen
Ptolemy

3. The rise of Rome from a small settlement, only a minor city-state under Etruscan control, into the empire which dominated all the Mediterranean world is an extraordinary historical feat. The myths of Romulus and Remus (see picture p. 52) and the literary description in Vergil's Aeneid, are important in establishing the Romans' view of themselves as worthy of such an accomplishment.

4. The fall of Rome, a process rather than a single event, deserves equally serious consideration. The authors rightly note the debate over the cause and do not fall into the trap of monocausation. To treat this topic properly, sections I, II and III of the next chapter may also be considered.

BOXES

BOX p. 55. "Slavery as Enforced Servitude" [closer look]. Written by the textbook authors to provide some perspective on slavery, not only in the Greco-Roman world, but on slavery in the Americas as well.

BOX p. 62. "The Destruction of Pompeii" [written record]. A primary source on the sudden annihilation of the people of a thriving city by an erupting volcano. The accompanying photo of a grisly body makes a dramatic pair of documents, written and physical.

BOX p. 64. "Menu for a Roman Banquet" [written record]. You might have someone read this aloud, and see what kind of reactions you get from the students. Personally, I'd hate to have to eat a roast parrot. Historically, what kind of society could afford to feed its elites like this?

BOX p. 68. "The Satyricon" [written record]. By the same token, ask you students if they can imagine people eating the foods from the above menu, then being suitably bored by entertainments such as those satirized here.

Now let us turn to the specific subheadings of the chapter for consideration of several important details.

I. THE REPUBLIC
&
II. CRISIS OF THE REPUBLIC

The growth of Rome from a minor city state to a major power is recounted here, along with a description of the social and political structure of the Republic. Students who think that Roman history is alien to them might be surprised to note how many of the words and concepts they recognize: senate, censor, phalanx, legion, and crossing the river Rubicon.

Hannibal's elephants and the Punic Wars should catch the imagination of many students. The MAP should introduce students to the concept of a "Mediterranean civilization," while Western Europe was no more than a barbarian frontier to the North. Tacitus opined that the Germanic tribes were of pure blood, because no foreigners would ever settle there--the weather was so terrible.

The crises of the Republic have long been used as object lessons of what happens when governors lose sight of the good of their people and rule selfishly. And indeed the common people themselves can be equally selfish and short sighted, looking only to their own desires, and being unwilling to sacrifice for the common good. The stories of Julius Caesar, Mark Antony, and Cleopatra should be retold, for they form part of our common culture.

The color pictures, particularly the one of the law student (or baker) and his wife on page 67, provide vivid windows into the past. Students should be encouraged to ask questions based upon them, and speculate about what the people and their lives were really like.

TO DEFINE AND DISCUSS:
praetor
tribunes
Carthage
Hannibal and Scipio Africanus
Roman slavery
the Gracchus brothers
Octavian
Brutus.

III. THE ROMAN EMPIRE
&
IV. RELIGION, WRITING, AND THOUGHT

One of the major elements in the success of the Roman Empire was the rather wide extension of Roman citizenship, and the relatively equitable application of Roman law. Students should be helped to understand this fact, perhaps by making reference to the following chapter's account of the spread of Christianity among the Roman citizens of the far-flung empire.

Military force was important as well. One reason the Empire lasted was that its enemies were unable to put as many men in the field as the Romans. Subject peoples, like the barbarians to the North and the Jews in Palestine, were able to win battles against individual Roman units, but the Empire had the wealth, organizational ability, and discipline to marshall its forces and reestablish its rule repeatedly for several hundred years.

Yet the very size of the Empire contributed to its undoing, and the attempts by Diocletian and others to decentralize the government and still retain its unity were not very successful.

In recent years substantial progress has been made in the study of women's and social history, and this information is reflected in the new edition. Students may wish to discuss the life styles and circumstances of the women and of slaves, comparing Greek and Roman society.

Roman culture derived much from the Greeks, and two good ways to point this out is to show the relationship between Greek and Roman religion and also between Greek and Roman art and architecture.

TO DEFINE AND DISCUSS:
imperator
Messianic
Claudius
Trajan's Column
Pliny (elder and younger)
Pompeii
tetrarchy
Constantine
Caesarean birth

SUMMATION

One of the problems with any survey textbook, and any survey course, is that time is collapsed for the students. They need to be reminded that the rise and fall of Rome was a process of a good half a millennium, even though it is covered in a single chapter. Later in the course a chapter may cover less than fifty years, one tenth as much time. Nevertheless, the majesty of Rome is well summarized here, and windows into the details of the civilization it embodied illuminate what life must have been like (like the mosaic of the gladiators). Myths are exploded (Nero did not fiddle while Rome burned), but the inadequacies and absurdities of the culture are not hidden from view. The students will have valuable foundations stones upon which to build their understanding of the future chapters.

CRITICAL THINKING

The heritage, or more correctly the multiple heritages, of the Greco-Roman world are lifted up for us and our students in the questions offered here. So many of our students are very present-minded, and sometimes we must exploit that present-mindedness to catch their interest. Thus you can use these questions to explore with them what aspects of Roman (and also Greek) society are still influencing us today. In culture (philosophy and architecture), in the uses of material power (engineering and war), in values and in law. A review of these critical thinking questions will prepare the students for answering the essay questions below.

4. JUDAISM AND CHRISTIANITY

The MAJOR GOAL of this chapter is to familiarize the students with the two major religious traditions of the West, and with their position in the Roman world. Much has been written lately about how textbooks have avoided the subject of religion in order to avoid offending some religious group or other. This book has pulled no punches in telling the history of these two religions, and their conflicts. Thus not everyone who has had a strong Jewish or Christian religious upbringing will recognize their own tradition here.

The NINTH EDITION follows the same topical structure as the previous one, but it has been shortened by deleting a number of factual details, interpretive comments, one BOX and some illustrations. For example, the long biblical quotation and the apologetic footnote accompanying it, on page 106 of the eighth edition are both gone. The chapter remains true to the general approach of the previous editions.

BASIC OBJECTIVES

1. The items mentioned in the chapter headings range from the commonly recognizable to the rather obscure; yet even those which seem obvious should be carefully discussed. Students raised outside the Judeo-Christian tradition may be meeting these items for the first time, and those who think they already know them, may not share a common understanding of them with others in the class.

astrology
cults: Cybele, Isis, Mithra
Judea
Jesus
Judaeo-Christians
Paul
gentile
pagan
Constantine
bishops
monasticism
Nicene Creed
Augustine

2. The students should recognize, or identify, or locate on a MAP, the following major items from the chapter.

Dionysus (Bacchus)
Stoics
Neoplatonism

Gospels
the Maccabees and Hanukkah
Hasadim
Sadducees and Pharisees
Dead Sea Scrolls and Essenes
Aramaic
episkopos
presbyter
St. Benedict
Eucharist
baptism
the seven sacraments
ecumenical
Vulgate
The City of God
free will and predestination

3. The authors attempt to make distinctions in this chapter between statements of <u>history</u> and statements of <u>faith</u>. That is not always easy to do, so when your students have trouble separating these two types of statements, please be patient. One way to do it is with the preparatory phrase "Christians believe . . ." or "Jews believe . . ." so that one need not get hung up on the issue of whether or not Jesus really did rise from the dead after three days, etc.

4. In many respects this is the most difficult and most important of the chapters so far. Students may know or care little about ancient Greece and Rome, but a great many of them know--or think they know--a great deal about Jesus and what he meant. If you are blessed with a pluralistic class, with Jews, Protestants of various hues, Catholics, Muslims, and people from various non-Western traditions, you will have the challenge and joy of putting American ideals of religious toleration into practice. If you have a more homogeneous group, you may wish to jar them from their own received truths by suggesting that there may be in this world some admirable people who believe differently than they do.

BOXES

BOX p. 76 "New Knowledge on Old Events" [doing history]. This new BOX on Ebla (which did not even make the index of the eighth edition) explains how new archaeological finds can revise our historical picture of the past. Students should get the idea that what we call history is not static, but a dynamic understanding of the world. You might wish to discuss with them what constitutes an historical "fact."

BOX p. 80 "Ecclesiastes on Transience" [written record]. The eighth edition calls this "...on Transience and history" and includes portions of chapter 3. Even this shorter BOX contains many well known lines, and the essence of the vanity of history, "there is no new thing under the sun." You might see how many of your students agree with this piece of biblical wisdom.

BOX p. 81 "Nero and the Christians" [written record]. This vivid description deserves to be analyzed by the students in some detail. It is important to note that Tacitus was often critical of his fellow Romans. Note his ironic comment that Rome was "where all things hideous and shameful from every part of the word find their center and become popular."

BOX p. 85 "The Rule of St. Benedict" [written record]. Note the combination of egalitarian and patriarchal concepts mixed into this portion of the rule. Students might consider how rules like this allowed monasticism to survive the fall of the Roman Empire and keep the candles of civilization during throughout the early middle ages.

Now let us turn to the specific subheadings of the chapter for consideration of several important details.

I. THE IMPORTANCE OF RELIGION IN THE LATER ROMAN WORLD
&
II. JUDEA

These two sections discuss the context into which Christianity was born. The authors have taken care to show how some of the attractive elements in Christianity had their parallels in the mystery cults of the Roman world, such as ritual meals, rites of purification through baptism (or other washing), and ideas of everlasting life. Some of your students may take umbrage at this, seeing it as part of the atheistic plot to undermine their religious beliefs in the name of "secular humanism." But others may be pleased to see the Bible quoted as a legitimate historical source.

It is important, I believe, to make the point that the writers of the Bible were not primarily writing history (or biography) but were writing religious documents. Such an approach may give solace to both the fundamentalists and the skeptics in your class, because it recognizes that it is not necessary to throw out the theological baby with the bathwater as soon as some bright fellow identifies a chronological inconsistency among the gospels. Use of the BOXES from the Bible, and introducing the concept of exegesis will help as well.

Finally, you may wish to attack explicitly the myth of deicide, which has burdened the relationship of Jews and Christians for centuries. Catholic and mainline Protestant theologians now agree that it is inaccurate and pernicious to blame the crucifixion of Jesus, the Christ, on THE JEWS as a whole. The textbook account makes this clear, though it avoids explicit discussion of the deicide myth and its implications.

TO DEFINE AND DISCUSS:
fortune and fate
carnal cults
Epicurus
logos
Hellenism

Hasmoneans
Herod
the chronological dates of Jesus
Messiah
sanhedrin
destruction of the Temple.

III. CHRISTIANITY IN THE PAGAN WORLD
&
IV. THE ORGANIZATION OF THE CHURCH

It may be useful for students to flip back to the previous chapter to recall the outlines of Roman political history as the context for the religious developments described here. Or, perhaps you are doing both chapters 3 and 4 as a single unit to emphasize the relationship. In either case it is important that the students realize that there is no simple way to separate church and state in the Roman world. [Perhaps it is not even so easily done in our own modern world.]

The stories of the martyrs who were persecuted by the anti-Christian emperors may be told by one of your students who has been raised in the tradition which emphasizes the saintly martyrs. If not, the BOX on Nero should provide graphic enough prose. The conversion of Constantine, just before a battle in a civil war, should remind the students of the close link between religion and secular power. This will provide essential background for the later discussions of the civil/religious relations during the middle ages.

The discussion of church organization may strike some of the students a trifle dull, but remind them how important such arrangements are in the practical world. Who controls the church buildings, the church lands, and the church budget? Does it simply become a business, for the profit of the priesthood, or is it kept pure and near the simplicity of the original Christian message? What of the tensions between the secular clergy, who work in the everyday world among the people, great and small, and the regular clergy, who take refuge in monasteries? Who will protect Christians from the men like Nero and Attila the Hun?

TO DEFINE AND DISCUSS:
Pliny the Younger and Trajan
"atheism"
Tertullian and toleration
Theodosius
Peter/*Petros*
St. Jerome
clergy and laity
the Coptic church
celibacy
St. Benedict and St. Basil

V. THE DEVELOPMENT OF CHRISTIAN THOUGHT
&
VI. THOUGHT AND LETTERS IN THE FIRST CHRISTIAN CENTURIES

Some of your students may quickly tire of the theological abstractions in these sections, particularly since they seem to be segregated near the end of the chapter and may come to the students' attention only when time is short or the wits are dimmed by long hours at the books. Yet these theological debates reflected the differences within the church which caused centuries of struggle, torture, and warfare.

Orthodoxy vs. heresy, of course, is not limited to Christian struggles. It seems that the most bitter of struggles are between siblings, often over apparently fine points of doctrine which now seem of little importance. Ask the students how many of them would split heads over Arianism or the monophysite heresy!

Perhaps this is the point which should be made: a religion which worships the God-Man called the Prince of Peace called forth great armies to fight over such theological differences.

Students should react more sympathetically to the story of Augustine of Hippo, who indulged in sexual and other pleasures as a youth, but became a great theologian and leader of the church. Even the theological issues he attacked seem more real, at least to my students: do we have free will, or are we predestined to become what we will become?

TO DEFINE AND DISCUSS:
the seven sacraments: baptism, confirmation, Eucharist, penance, extreme unction (rite for the dying, or anointing the sick), ordination, and marriage
Manichaean ideas
monophysites
St. Ambrose
Hippo
Pelagius
original sin

SUMMATION

Many authors define "The West" as that part of the world which was dominated by the Christian church. Others point out that the church was not so important for its purely religious message (i.e. the exact teachings of Jesus of Nazareth) but rather for the broader cultural ideas of Greece and Rome for which the Christian Church was a conduit, and for the artistic intellectual, and political systems which accompanied these Greco-Roman ideas. Thus the "Judaeo-Christian tradition" remains a major legacy for our modern world, however one worships, or whether one worships at all, in the world today.

CRITICAL THINKING

The origins of the Christianity, within the context of the Roman and the Jewish world of the first centuries A.D., is a topic of fascination on controversy. Critical thinking about such matters, which often touch on sensitive matters of religious faith, is not easy. Try to help your students to think like historians at this point, "checking their theological guns at the door." Their personal faith, I believe, is their own business. But they should have their historical facts as straight as they possibly can.

5. THE EARLY MIDDLE AGES IN WESTERN EUROPE

The MAJOR GOAL of this chapter is to familiarize the students with the civilization of the period which was once called the "Dark Ages." The term is still used for the period prior to the rise of ancient Greece, but it is out of favor for the middle ages. Calling the period "the dark ages" does not recognize the fact that substantial civilization remained after the fall of Rome.

THE NINTH EDITION of this chapter abridges the length by cutting some details, for example on Charlemagne, but the general outline and the interpretive framework remains unchanged. The BOXES on the Venerable Bede and Celtic Flowering have been deleted.

BASIC OBJECTIVES

1. All students should be familiar with the major items and concepts mentioned in the headings and subheadings of the chapter.

Visigoths, Vandals, Huns, Ostrogoths
Anglo-Saxon
the Northmen
Danes
Carolingian and Saxon Empires
feudalism
vassals
manorialism
vernacular
Beowulf

2. The students should be sufficiently familiar with other major items from the chapter to recognize them and describe the accurately.

barbarian
Celtic
Gaul
Acquitaine
Theodoric
Pepin
Pope Gregory the Great
Charles the Great (Charlemagne)
The Song of Roland
mosaics
Normans
Hugh Capet
fief
investiture
demesne
Capitulare

Vikings

3. Students should deal with the question of what constitutes a "dark age," and what constitutes "civilization." To a certain extent, the textbook to this point has presented a story of unfolding progress. Each successor civilization seemed to take major elements of the previous ones and use them to make major achievements of their own. Progress, in some sense, seemed inherent in history. Now, with the fall of Rome, things seem to take a step backwards. Why do today's scholars reject the term "dark ages"?

4. Much of the political and religious history of the period deals with leaders trying to preserve, or to reestablish, the old glory of imperial Rome. Charlemagne is the greatest example of this, but by no means the only one. The MAPS, which you can use as TRANSPARENCIES, will help you make this clear, as well as illustrate the general chaos of the barbarian invasions.

5. Whether you want to accept or challenge the textbook authors' contention that the early middle ages was a "dark age", you might make clear that one of the problems with studying the period is the relative dearth of written sources. In comparison to Classical Period, or the High Middle Ages and the Renaissance, the written remains of the early middle ages are very limited both in quantity and in kind. Much of the story of the Germanic and the Norse invasions has to be traced by looking for archaeological scraps of metal which have been left behind.

BOXES

BOX p. 97, "The Language of History: [doing history]. This BOX is a revised and extended version of one which was in the first chapter of the EIGHTH EDITION. It is an important interpretive commentary, particularly with today's sensitivity with regard to language, a topic which is by no means limited to the content of this chapter. This BOX would be very useful even if you do not use Chapter 5 in your assignments (for example, if you are skipping the early middle ages to concentrate on another period). The B.C./A.D. discussion really does fit here into the early middle ages, of course. It might be expanded by introducing the students to C.E. (= the Common Era = A.D.) and B.C.E. (= Before the Common Era = B.C.). Your students may run into that usage in some of their other history books.

BOX p. 107 "Life in the Country" [written record]. The BOX has been abbreviated by deleting several items, but that might make it even more useful for focussing discussion. You might ask which of your students has personal experience with farm life, and have them tease out some comparisons between their experience and the descriptions implied here. For those concerned about women's studies, you might ask about the perceived gender roles. For those with interests in law and government, you might raise the question of the role of government in preventing poverty.

BOX p. 109 "Slavery in the Early Middle Ages" [written record]. American students do (and should) have an interest in the institutions of slavery. This BOX will help to put that interest in perspective

BOX p. 111 "Beowulf" [written record]. Many of your students, no doubt, will have encountered Beowulf in English classes, and the portion here will provide a good opportunity to make and reinforce links between disciplines.

Now let us turn to the specific subheadings of the chapter for consideration of several important details.

I. THE BREAKDOWN OF ROMAN CIVILIZATION

We return again to the question of the fall of Rome, this time looking at it from yet another angle, stressing the power of the "barbarian" invaders. Students should consider the timely question of whether wealthy and self-satisfied civilizations can stand the stresses placed on them by the pressures of have-not peoples who are willing to risk all in fighting for their future.

Students will doubtless ask for a date of "when Rome fell" and the sack of the city in 455 by the Vandals is a pretty good one to choose. But the textbook does a good job of showing that the transition was a slow one lasting over 100 years. Students must also remember that the Eastern Empire, at Byzantium, discussed in the next chapter, lived on.

TO DEFINE AND DISCUSS:
Goths
the battle of Adrianople
Germanic tribes
Emperor Zeno
Atilla the Hun.

II. THE FRANKS: THE BUILDING OF AN EMPIRE
&
III. AFTER CHARLEMAGNE: THE NORTHMEN

Charlemagne has a central position in the history of this period. He is claimed by both the French and the Germans as the "father" of their countries, and in a sense both claims are correct. More appropriate, however, is the claim by the European unity movement of the post-1945 era that Charlemagne was the precursor of a Europe which moved beyond mere nationalism. Compare the MAP of his empire with any map of the European Community today.

Yet the Carolingian Empire did not last beyond the century of Carlos Magnus himself. The pressures were too great from the outside, with contending invaders, and there was no institutionalization of the power of the state. Indeed, this may be a very good time to point out to the students what happens when there is virtually no state structure, but only personal government.

TO DEFINE AND DISCUSS:
Charles Martel
the Lombards
Pepin the Short
the Donation of Pepin
Einhard
Aachen
the Strasbourg Oaths of 842
the Norse voyages to the new world
Edward the Confessor
the *Danegeld*
the Saxon emperors
Europe in 1000.

IV. FEUDAL EUROPE
&
V. THE CIVILIZATION OF THE EARLY MIDDLE AGES IN THE WEST

Most of your students probably think that a Europe divided into national states is the "natural" condition of things, and that some form of central government, either tyrannical or free, has long been standard practice. They know the old saying that "nothing is certain but death and taxes." In the middle ages, however, there were no recognizable national states, indeed there was hardly any form of central government at all. There were no certain taxes--money rarely changed hands for any purpose. Death was so common as to be almost unimportant, because all believing Christians held that earthly existence was inevitably followed by eternal life--hopefully in heaven.

A window on this unfamiliar world is provided by the BOXES which describe common beliefs and practices, and by the pictures of the almost ghostly carvings which have survived.

TO DEFINE AND DISCUSS:
feudal contract
wardship
leige lord
serfdom
franklins
medieval slavery
Boethius
crypts
Sidonius Apollinaris
hagiographies
"Carolingian Renaissance"
funeral ships
Byzantine and Western art

SUMMATION

As the professor in charge of your course, you may or may not wish to follow the professors who wrote this textbook in rejecting the term "dark ages" for this period. Surely the civilization which it created, protected, and bequeathed to us was as admirable as any in history, if only because the circumstances which it had to endure were so terrible. We owe much to the scribes who labored in the Carolingian *scriptorium* and to the political and military leaders who protected them from the surrounding chaos. But your students should also have some appreciation for the reasons that other scholars and commentators have compared the entire age unfavorably with either the ancient civilizations of Greece and Rome on the one hand, or the Italian Renaissance (or even the High Middle Ages) on the other. To even out all civilizations as equally creative and praiseworthy may do justice to some unfairly maligned geniuses of the early middle ages, but it may confuse students who need to see the clear outlines of the peaks and valleys of the history they are studying for the first time.

CRITICAL THINKING

The concept of the "middle ages" was so problematical for the scholars and teachers developing the "world history standards" that they left it out altogether. For the purposes the study of Western Civilization, it makes sense in the traditional division between Ancient and Modern. Thus it is "middle" but it is not "mid-evil." You might wish to raise the question of periodization with your students.

6. BYZANTIUM AND ISLAM

The MAJOR GOAL of this chapter is to familiarize the students with two major competitors of Western Christian civilization, the Eastern Orthodox Christianity we name after the city of Byzantium, and Islamic (Muslim) civilization. During the early Middle Ages each of these civilizations was superior to the West in terms of economic and military power, and in terms of sophisticated education and learning. A major theme of the next several chapters of this book, implicitly or explicitly, is the growth in power of Western civilization at the expense of these two civilizations of the middle east.

The EIGHTH EDITION added significant material on women and family in Byzantine civilization and on the nature of Islam. The NINTH EDITION shortened the text by deleting a number of details and by streamlining transitional passages. One BOX was moved to Chapter 8. the BOX on the Koran was deleted.

Because the two subjects of this chapter are so different, this chapter of the INSTRUCTOR'S MANUAL will take a different form from the previous ones, treating the two portions separately.

BASIC OBJECTIVES CONCERNING BYZANTIUM

1. Every student should show some familiarity with the major items mentioned in the chapter headings and in the text itself.

Byzantium, Istanbul, Constantinople, Tsargrad
Imperator, Basileus, and Autocrat
Justinian's Code
Theophilus
Venice
barbarians
icon
iconoclasm
Caesaropapism
schism of 1054
Cyrillic alphabet
the Slavs
Varangian/Scandinavian
conversion of Vladimir, 980's
Kiev
Hagia Sophia

2. The term "Byzantine" has come to be used as a negative term signifying complexity and intrigue. You might discuss with the students just why that is so. The highly organized and stylized etiquette of the

court may help to explain it, but so might the fact that the history and politics of this civilization has been relatively little studied by westerners, so it appears more complex and impenetrable than it perhaps was in reality.

3. Students might be led to consider just why the split occurred between Western and Eastern Christendom. Was it merely the result of the administrative division of the Roman Empire? Was it a reflection of deep-seated differences reaching back to the ancient Greeks and Romans? Were the Westerners really "barbarians" in comparison with the sophisticates of the East?

4. Your students have already learned that Rome "fell" sometime in the fifth century. Now you can show them that it lived on, in a somewhat different form, for another thousand years. The chapter has a good deal of positive things to say about the Byzantine civilization, a useful antidote to the negative attitude (or silence) which characterize most approaches to the subject.

BOXES

BOX p. 117, "Theophilus on Justice" [written record]. Student's might consider both the abstract concept of justice represented in these stories, and the problem of whether justice ultimately comes from just laws or just persons.

BOX p. 119, "Dazzling the Barbarian" [written record]. Note who is the barbarian here, and the wealth and sophistication of the Byzantine Empire implied in the description. Compare also with the quotations from documents on p. 121.

BOX p. 127, "The Story of Ioasaph" [closer look]. This paraphrase and analysis of a hagiographic story can be compared to the "written record" sources on a couple of levels. First, the story itself is important for understanding Eastern Christianity. Second, the authors go on to engage in some comparative history. The use of "stories"--or "discourse" for historical analysis is very much in fashion with the post-modernists.

BASIC OBJECTIVES CONCERNING ISLAM

1. Students should recognize and demonstrate their familiarity with the major terms used in this portion of the chapter.

Muhammad
Islam
Muslims
"Mohammadanism"
Arabs
Mecca
the Koran
Ramadan

the hajj
the Hegira
jihad
Charles Martel and the battle of Tours
caliph
Shi'ite
Sunnite
Seljuk Turks
Arab science and mathematics
the Arabian Nights

2. This chapter, which limits itself to the period before the crusades (eleventh century), demonstrates the rapid growth of Islam after its founding by Muhammad in the 7th century. See the MAP. Students can graphically see how Islam comes to dwarf the Byzantine Empire, to which the first two thirds of the chapter was devoted.

3. In spite of the fact that much of this Islamic expansion was through conquest, the textbook tends to underplay the military aspect of this growth and emphasizes the fact that the Islamic rulers were relatively tolerant of Christians and Jews under their rule, recognizing them as fellow "people of the Book."

4. The disunity which grew among the Muslims, largely for political reasons, should be important to your students, who may have [should have] heard of the split between the Shi'ite and the Sunni branches, and the bitter disputes between them. Without being drawn into too much discussion of contemporary politics at this point, you may wish to note that fundamentalists of the Shi'ite group form the spearhead of Islamic radicalism today.

BOXES

BOX p. 133, "The Calamities of Love" [written record]. Since many of your students may be at the stage of their lives in which they are trying to make sense out of love relationships, this BOX might provide some useful discussion. How much of it reflects elements specific to medieval Islam, and how much is more universal?

Because the BOX on the Koran has been deleted, you may wish to supplement your discussion of that major document with an outside source, or return to the EIGHTH EDITION, p. 173, if you have it handy.

SUMMATION

This textbook, reflecting older models, still places substantially more emphasis on Byzantine civilization than on Islam. As you teach your course, you might wish to consider if this balance is the appropriate one for your students, given the importance of the resurgence of Islamic states today. Yet the importance of Greek orthodox Christianity, especially as it was bequeathed to the Slavs and still survives in Russia, should not be ignored. During the late 1980's the Soviet Union celebrated Vladimir's conversion from paganism to Christianity, and the collapse of Communism in the 1990's has inspired a renewed interest in Orthodox religion.

CRITICAL THINKING

Many of these questions are comparative in nature, and thus relate not only to this chapter but to the surrounding ones as well. That is good, because students too often learn (memorize) information in clumps, passing their exams, and then purging themselves to move on to the next clump. These questions move beyond that level, to higher thinking skills.

7. CHURCH AND SOCIETY IN THE MEDIEVAL WEST

The MAJOR GOAL of this chapter is to familiarize the students with the religious life of the Middle Ages in Western and Central Europe, and the implications of the power of the Church for the Holy Roman Empire, though that term is not emphasized. The following chapter covers roughly the same chronological period, but deals more specifically with the developments in France and Britain. The authors make a point of noting the importance of new information and interpretations which have born fruit over the past thirty years. Generally speaking, this "new history" has diminished the emphasis on the Renaissance as the birth of the modern world, and has argued that "the past is one long continuum in which the Middle Ages are no less relevant" to us than more recent times.

The NINTH EDITION makes few changes in this chapter, abbreviating some of the material and shortening the transitions. New material is added on Hildegard of Bingen.

BASIC OBJECTIVES

1. Students should know what the authors mean by the major terms in the chapter headings and subheadings.

the Church Universal
papal monarchy
the Investiture Controversy
Frederick Barbarossa
Innocent III
Augustinians
Cistercians
Dominican Friars
Franciscan Friars
Thomas Aquinas
mysticism

2. Students should be familiar with the other major terms, persons, and places developed in the chapter.

bourg, burgh, burg
the just price
courtly love
Mariolatry
"the gentle class"
medieval Jews
excommunication/interdict
Benedictine monastery at Cluny

Saxon Dynasty
King of Germany/Holy Roman Emperor
Hildebrand, Pope Gregory VII
Canossa
Hohenstaufen dynasty
German particularism
Francis of Assisi
universitas
nominalist/realist controversy
Scholasticism
Romanesque and Gothic styles
Giotto

3. Many of today's students dismiss the Middle Ages as a time of superstition and oppression, a "dark age" in all but name (and sometimes they still use the name). You have the challenge to overcome this prejudice and point out the rich variety of life during that era, the practical progress that was made (like inventing windmills), and--perhaps--even the sublime commitment which is represented by this "age of faith." The authors have given you some help here, by indicating in the BOXES some idea of life among medieval people, and by the beautiful color illustrations of the medieval cathedrals.

4. Students who are politically concerned might be drawn into a discussion (or debate) at this point on the question of the separation of church and state. The authors point out correctly that such separation was unthinkable in the Middle Ages (and indeed in the previous periods as well). Students might be drawn into the discussion by listing on the board the advantages of unity between church and state. Then they might look at the chaotic Investiture struggle to see evidence of the problems caused by this linkage.

5. Consider the MAPS in the book, or the TRANSPARENCIES to get an idea of the concepts of state, church, and nation during this period. Important is the fact that the maps have little relationship to the maps of the nations states of Europe later in the book.

BOXES

BOX p. 138, "Women of the Gentle Class" [written record]. Note how both class and gender tend to determine proper behavior. Is there an implication that the women of the common people would have behaved very differently?

BOX p. 140, "The Good Wife" [written record]. Students would do well to compare this with the "gentle class" women. Clearly this is the role of the middle class woman, with a hard working merchant husband. If both the husband and wife go out into the world to earn their living, who performs the tasks here assigned to the "good wife"?

BOX p. 151, "Knowledge That Is Lost" [doing history]. Students often get the idea that all history is progress. It is wise to consider what happens when this is not so.

Now let us turn to the specific subheadings of the chapter for consideration of several important details.

I. THE SOCIETY AND ITS ECONOMY
&
II. THE MEDIEVAL CHURCH AS INSTITUTION

It is important that the students get a solid idea of the three levels of society in medieval Europe, the clergy, the nobility, and "those who worked." These "estates" will be with us till the French Revolution. But, in addition, we now know that the <u>rise of the bourgeoisie</u> was already beginning, a force which still determines social history today. Discuss with them the roles of the various groups of society, men and women, slave and free, serf and nobleman, Christian and Jew. The Inquisition and the heretics, which you might expect to have introduced here actually appear in the next chapter.

TO DEFINE AND DISCUSS:
"the state"
the decline of slavery
law merchant
bills of exchange
canon law
auctoritas and *potestas*.

III. THE INVESTITURE CONTROVERSY
&
IV. PAPACY AND EMPIRE, 1152-1273

Purists may argue that this massive struggle was not a conflict between church and state, because both sides theoretically recognized the ideal of an order ordained by God and ruled with two swords, secular and ecclesiastical. But for the purposes of an introductory course that reasoning may be a bit sophisticated (if not actually sophistical). Students should be brought to realize, among all the Henries, Gregories, and Fredericks, that the Pope and the Emperor both wanted to control the church in the Empire, for it was a mighty institution for both religious and secular purposes. Moreover, it was in part this costly struggle which weakened the Empire and made it virtually impossible to turn into a modern state. In the next chapter we will see how the French kings controlled the church in their territories, making much easier the unification of modern France.

TO DEFINE AND DISCUSS:
teutonici
cardinals
Emperor Henry IV
"concordat"
the Welf (Guelf) vs. Hohenstaufen (Ghibelline) feud

Frederick II Hohenstaufen

V. THE CHURCH IN SOCIETY

The authors avoid the phrase "age of faith" when describing the Middle Ages, perhaps because it has become something of a cliché. But your students may not know that it is a cliché, so you may wish to introduce them to the concept. On the other hand, they should realize that a society which could construct the superb Gothic churches at Amiens and Chartres, with all their technical and artistic accomplishments, was by no means a crude or uncivilized society. Faith could bind humankind together for high goals. Make good use of the pictures in the textbook, and supplement them with slides or a visit to a neogothic local site, however modest. Giotto is well described in the book, but you will have to use your own resources to show much of his art to your class.

TO DEFINE AND DISCUSS:
Cluny
Citeax
St. Bernard of Clairvaux
St. Francis of Assisi
the seven liberal arts
Peter Abelard (you might add Helioise)
Averroes
the syllogism
John of Salisbury
law of nature (get your PRELAW students involved)
flying buttresses (not well illustrated)
statuary as didactic material

SUMMATION

If you have had the opportunity to travel among medieval castles and cathedrals you have the recollections to introduce your students to the extraordinary world of the high Middle Ages. But you also know how difficult it is to communicate, wither by words or by pictures, the soaring beauty of the Gothic and everything it stood for. Some of your students may have a romanticized grasp of the fantastic nature of this civilization, and you can draw on that. For others, I'm afraid, all you can do is to teach them some of the facts and vocabulary, which will rest unused in some backwater of their minds until one day circumstances will suddenly make that half forgotten history suddenly meaningful. The middle ages lasted a thousand years, more or less, and it still has much to teach us if we can give it a chance.

CRITICAL THINKING

Recently there has been a flury of activity recreating "medieval" life, legend, and warfare. Some of it is volunteer (Society for Creative Anachronism) some of it rather commercial. Perhaps the Middle Ages are not so far from our own age as we sometime think. The questions here, nevertheless, can help to bridge the gaps in time (and approach) between that time and our own.

8 THE BEGINNINGS OF THE SECULAR STATE

The MAJOR GOAL of this chapter is to familiarize the students with the origins of the modern national state, as exemplified in the English and French monarchies of the high Middle Ages. Associated with these two states is the growth in vernacular non-religious literature. Implicit in the chapter is the idea that "the West" is somehow ahead of the rest of European civilization in the progress toward the modern democratic nation-state.

In the NINTH EDITION this chapter is somewhat shortened, though the overall approach is the same. Three BOXES have been cut, along with a quotation for the Domesday Book. One BOX has been inserted, Ibn Khaldun on error in history, relocated from Chapter 6.

BASIC OBJECTIVES

1. All students should be able to demonstrate their familiarity with the major concepts and individuals mentioned in the chapter's headings and subheadings.

secular state
Capetians
St. Louis
Philip the Fair
the Norman Conquest
Henry I and Henry II
Richard I and John
Magna Carta
Parliament
Edward I

2. The students should be able to recognize and discuss the other major items in the chapter.

Ile de France
Albigensians
Inquisition
Parlement de Paris
bourgeois
Estates-General
Pope Boniface VIII
a papal bull
Unum Sanctum
William the Conqueror
the Bayeux Tapestry
the Domesday Book
the Angevin Empire
Thomas a Becket
Roger Bacon

chivalry
The Song of Roland
Dante's *Divine Comedy*
Chaucer's *Canterbury Tales*

2. In several respects this chapter parallels the previous one, but concentrates on the English and French regions, rather than central Europe. In each case secular monarchs struggled for power with each other and with the papacy for political, economic, and cultural domination. But note the clear difference in emphasis--Chapter 7's title cites the Church, and Chapter 8's the Secular State. Students should realize that in each case religion was very important; it was, after all, the "age of faith." But in both England and France the monarchs were generally able to gain local control from the papacy, though neither challenged papal rule over the church universal in a theoretical sense.

4. The first sentence in the chapter refers to "those lands which became France and England." You may wish to stress the point that although we tend to refer to medieval "France" and "England" as if they were modern national states, in reality they were not. The dynasties moved back and forth across the channel pursing their family and territorial ambitions without any reference to English or French nationalities. This continues to be true into through the Hundred Years War, discussed in Chapter 10.

5. The words <u>parliament</u> and <u>parlement</u> are introduced in this chapter to describe British and French institutions respectively. Be sure your students know the differences between them. Some may see this as nit picking, but your PRE-LAW students will quickly see the importance of the distinction. With such terms as <u>entail</u> and <u>quo warranto</u> salted throughout the chapter, such young men and women should have a field day picking up concepts and vocabulary which (they think) will sometime make them rich.

5. Note the repeated, though rather oblique, references to the crusades in this chapter and the preceding one. Your students should be made sensitive to the important role of Islam, and to the conflicts between Judeo-Christian and Muslim civilizations (extending into the late twentieth century). The crusades will be dealt with systematically in Chapter 9.

BOXES

BOX p. 162, "Sources of Error" [doing history]. This is a primary source, so it might also be classified as "the written word." It has wandered here from the chapter on Islam, perhaps because it fits the chronlogy better in this chapter. In any case, it is useful for some paragraph by paragraph unpacking with your students. Do they simply think the textbook is always right?

BOX p. 167, "Magna Carta" [written record]. Ask your students if they have ever seen a copy of this wonderful document on display--there are copies that tour sometimes. Then, work with them to see how far we have come since King John's (and Robin Hood's) day.

BOX p. 170, "The Song of Roland" [written record]. Compare the story here with the chapter on Charlemagne for the students. Chivalry is important here, but so are standard tales of heroism in war.

Now let us turn to the specific subheadings of the chapter for consideration of several important details.

I. THE DEVELOPMENT OF FRANCE: FROM HUGH CAPET TO PHILIP THE FAIR

The glory of the French monarchy, and the crushing defeat it suffers during the great French Revolution, provides one of the major subplots of the textbook, from this chapter through chapter 18. American students, particularly those living in the vast portions of the United States which were once part of the French Empire, owe more to the French heritage than they probably realize. Ask them to identify <u>St. Louis</u>, and they will no doubt cite an American city rather than a medieval French king. The PHOTO of the stained glass of his chapel in Paris in no way does it justice, but it gives your students a glimpse of the splendor for which the French monarchy is responsible, and you can follow up later with the Louvre and Versailles.

TO DEFINE AND DISCUSS:
suzerain
curia regis
viscounts
Waldensians
sénéchal
the papacy at Avignon.

II. THE DEVELOPMENT OF ENGLAND

Among the few dates which should be firmly imprinted on the mind of every student of history is <u>1066</u>. The Norman conquest is not only an excellent story, but it forms part of the shared heritage we have with our British cultural cousins. Indeed our language itself was established by the mix of Anglo-Saxon and Norman French which was created by this conquest. [Tell your students that the common folk used Anglo-Saxon, i.e. Germanic, terms, like HOUSE, while the new overlords used French terms, like MANSION, for their greater dwellings.] But even the powerful Norman kings could not impose a permanent tyranny. Rather they developed a tradition of the rule of law and consultation with the "peers" of the realm, which eventually grew into the liberty and justice for all, which we hold dear. There is something of the "Whig" myth in all of this, no doubt. But it is an important myth, with which your students must be familiar, even if you, and they, wish to view it critically in the long run.

TO DEFINE AND DISCUSS:
Battle of Hastings
The Anglo-Saxon Chronicle
exchequer
jury/verdict
Richard "The Lionhearted"
scutage
Mortmain
Oxford University
"the English Justinian"

III. SCIENCE AND LITERATURE IN THE WEST

The authors have already introduced the argument that the Middle Ages was not merely an age of darkness and superstition, and that argument is carried on here by specific reference to the discoveries of late medieval science and technology, particularly the rationality of Roger Bacon (not to be confused with Sir Francis Bacon, nearly 400 years later). Vernacular literature supports this argument. Both Chaucer and Dante (who has wandered here from the Renaissance chapter) dealt with religious themes, but from a secular--and thus "modern"--point of view.

TO DEFINE AND DISCUSS:
Charlemagne and Roland
Eleanor of Aquitaine
King Arthur
courtly love
Dante's Beatrice
Chaucer and Canterbury

SUMMATION

American students may come into your classroom assuming that England and France have always been natural allies, since they shared the heritage of the West, in more or less "pure form," and they fought as allies is World Wars I and II. You now have the opportunity to show them that these two great countries--even back in the Middle Ages--were not only rivals, but often at war with one another. You can take your students, through your class presentations and the material in this book, from the Battle of Hastings through the burning of Joan of Arc during the Hundred Years War, to Quebec, and Waterloo. In many respects it has been a most creative tension, and we can enjoy the fruits of its creativity without suffering the brutalities which accompanied it over the centuries.

CRITICAL THINKING

The parallelism, both in terms of chronlogy and in terms of the issues, with the privious chapter is very clear. There is ample opportunity to get students to do some comparitive history here, noting the similarities and differences between the Anglo-French, and the Germanic Middle Ages. Be sure to use the MAPS to show how even the borders were very different.

9. THE LATE MIDDLE AGES IN EASTERN EUROPE

The MAJOR GOAL of this chapter is to familiarize the students with the developments in the Byzantine Empire, in the area we now call the Middle East, and in Russia, during the Middle Ages and the early modern period. The events in this part of the world were partly interlocked with those of Western Europe, and partly very separate. The general period in question is from the eleventh century to the seventeenth century, extending well beyond the period we think of as medieval. To help your students get a sense of time and place, use a TIME LINE and the MAPS to emphasize the overlapping relationship of the material in this chapter with that in prior and succeeding chapters.

For the EIGHTH EDITION some material was added on the later Crusades and the decline of the Byzantine Empire. For the NINTH EDITION many of the paragraphs have been abbreviated by eliminating certain details, and a few transitional paragraphs have been eliminated. A BOX on the fall of Constantinople to the Turks has been replaced by one on the Crusades. The overall approach and interpretation is unchanged.

BASIC OBJECTIVES

1. Every student should know about the major items mentioned in the chapter's headings and subheadings.

the Crusades
military orders
Muslim reconquest
Byzantium
the Latin Empire
Ottoman Turks
Tatars
Muscovite
Ivan the Terrible
the zemski sobor

2. Students should show some recognition and understanding of the other major items and concepts introduced in the chapter.

relics and pilgrimages
indulgences
Templars, Hospitalers, and Teutonic Knights
Saladin
the Children's Crusade
theocentric
Venice
millets
janissaries
Suleiman the Magnificent

Lithuania
Novgorod
Genghis Kahn
the Romanov dynasty
the Cossacks
the Kremlin

3. In certain respects you are leading your students into alien territory when you move to the East and Southeast from the traditional centers of Western Civilization. Much of the chapter deals with wars and repressions. Christian fights Muslim, Latin fights Greek, and Russians Asian hordes and establish an inward-looking autocracy, suspicious of Western influences. This information helps students to understand the background of many of the conflicts of the late twentieth century between states with a Western Judeo-Christian heritage and Islamic states.

4. But you should also give the students some appreciation of these Eastern civilizations for their own sake. The Crusaders are realistically portrayed; some may have been saints, but the majority seemed to have behaved like mighty sinners. The Byzantines are weak, but they struggle to hold together their empire, and do so for hundreds of years. Russia inherits the mantle (literally, see the description of the crowning of the czars) of Byzantium, and establishes itself as a rough and ready state in a hostile environment.

BOXES

BOX p. 174, "The Crusades" [closer look]. An interpretive essay carrying on the thread of the use of loaded language in historical description. To use the term "crusade" now is to take on the aura of a holy war, one blessed by God for a high moral purpose. Ask your students when they have heard the word "crusade" used in the news, or in political discourse.

BOX p. 175, "Pope Urban at Clermont" [written record]. This proclamation rings dramatically even today. If you have a student who has acting experience, you might have that student read this aloud. And (if it does not strike you as too corny) plant a response with a few students: "God wills it! God wills it!"

BOX p. 180, "The Sack of Constantinople" [written record]. After the high moral and religious drama of Pope Urban's call, this record provides a cold splash of realism. Ask your students if they know of other instances when soldiers go off to war preaching a lofty cause, only to descend to barbarism.

Now let us turn to the specific subheadings of the chapter for consideration of several important details.

I. THE CRUSADES

The very term "crusade" carries with it a sense of religious mission and moral worth. Eisenhower called his memoirs of World War II *Crusade in Europe*. But the crusaders, on the whole, do not emerge as very admirable in this chapter; indeed, the authors once refer to them as "human locusts." To bring balance to the students' picture, you may wish to stress the idealism of Pope Urban and the relatively enlightened policies of Emperor Frederick II. The intellectual and economic impact of contact with the East is also a positive aspect of the Crusades.

TO DEFINE, LOCATE, AND DISCUSS:
Christ's Passion
True Cross
Asia Minor
Anatolia
plenary indulgence
poll tax
Edessa
Saladin
Antioch
Tyre
Emperor Frederick II
Acre
Gaza
bazaar
tariff
damask
the Iberian "crusade"
Toledo

II. THE FALL OF BYZANTIUM, 1081-1453
&
III. THE OTTOMAN EMPIRE, 1453-1699

These two chapter segments sweep for more than six centuries, and it would be a good idea to remind the students how long that really was (in comparison to the history of Europeans in the Americas, for example), even though it is dealt with in only a few pages in the book, and probably fewer minutes in class. To get an even greater perspective, have them flip back to the MAPS to compare the Byzantine-Roman Empire, the Ottoman Turkish Empire, and Alexander's conquests some 1800 years before. Finally, you may wish to remind them (if the current newspapers do not) of the ongoing tensions between Greeks and Turks in the region today.

TO DEFINE, LOCATE, AND DISCUSS:
the Comneian dynasty
the Latin Emperors of Byzantium
the Mongols
Timur the Lame (Tamerlane)
Armenia
millet
the tribute of male children
janissaries

gunpowder and artillery
sages (*ulema*)
Belgrade
the Habsburgs
the sieges of Vienna (1529 and 1683)

IV. RUSSIA
FROM THE THIRTEENTH TO THE END OF THE SEVENTEENTH CENTURY

Because of the political tensions which are generally described as the Cold War, historians had a delicate and especially important task when teaching Americans about Russia. It was easy to portray it as a backward and barbaric country, cut off from the West in part by geography and in part by its own choice. Surely there is much evidence to support that interpretation in this chapter. On the other hand, it would be quite wrong to portray Russia as a natural enemy of the West. The czars consciously sought to link themselves with the tradition of the Roman Empire (Czar=Caesar), and in the 1980's even the Communist government celebrated the coming of Christianity to Slavic Europe a thousand years ago.

TO DEFINE, LOCATE, AND DISCUSS:
Lithuania and Poland
the *veche* (town council)
the Volga
the "Tatar yoke"
Kazan
Czargrad (or Tsargrad, Constantinople)
the service nobility
the *oprichnina*
Boris Godunov
the "Time of Troubles"
the patriarch
Old Church Slavonic
the Kremlin
St. Basil's Cathedral
trade with England and Holland

SUMMATION

At this point it might be useful to pause and recall the pivotal role of the great city state, Venice. It was a key link between the West and the East. Venetian merchants benefited from this relationship, sometimes constructively, sometimes in an exploitive fashion, but the wealth they garnered created an exquisite city, and contributed to the flowering of the Renaissance.

More important, however, is Jerusalem, and you might use this opportunity to turn your students' attention to this "Holy City." give us a glimpse of this city during the crusades. But ask your students to look backwards and forwards, back to the establishment of the Temple under Solomon two thousand years earlier, and the life of Jesus at the turn from B.C. to A.D., and forward to the struggles between Israeli Jews and Palestinian Muslims and Christians today. During the high Middle Ages Christian knights conquered the city, slew its inhabitants, and held it for more than a century. They in turn were driven out by the sword of Islam. Think of the blood which has been shed upon the streets of that city on a hill, holy to Judaism, Islam, and Christianity.

CRITICAL THINKING

This chapter deals with three great and powerful empires, the Byzantine, the Ottoman, and the Russian. During the many centuries encompassed by the chapter the Byzantine Empire faltered and fell. The Ottoman Empire defeated the Byzantine, advanced into Europe to the very gates of Vienna, and then began its decline. And the Russian Empire began from humble origins, took its place as the "Third Rome," and rose to great power status. There is plenty of material here for critical thinking about the rise and fall of powerful empires.

10. THE RISE OF THE NATION

The MAJOR GOAL of this chapter is to introduce the students to what historians call the modern world, the world of secular values, national states, and progress. The chapter also describes the decline of the world of the high Middle Ages, which rotted like an overly ripe fruit left upon the tree. The contrast between the rise of national monarchies in England, France, and Spain, and the perpetuation of feudal forms and decentralization in the German and Italian states has already been hinted at in the contrast between chapters 8 and 7. To introduce this chapter to your students you may wish to recall that earlier dichotomy.

The NINTH EDITION has shortened some of the paragraphs by deleting details and transitional commentaries and cut two of the BOXES and some of the pictures. Substantial new material has been added on women in late medieval society, particularly the social and economic rights. Some scholars, the authors point out, see a kind of "golden age" for women in the fourteenth and fifteenth centuries.

BASIC OBJECTIVES

1. All students should demonstrate an understanding of the major concepts named in the chapter's headings and subheadings.

Hundred Years' War
Estates General
Burgundians and Armagnacs
bastard feudalism
Lancaster and York
particularism
the Empire
condottieri

2. Students should also show an understanding of the other major concepts, names and places, important for the chapter.

Black Death/bubonic plague
Valois dynasty
Jacquerie
Joan of Arc
Gallicanism
Charles the Bold of Burgundy
Piers Plowman
Wars of the Roses
Tudor dynasty
Granada
the *Cortes*

Ferdinand and Isabella
Habsburg dynasty
electoral princes
the Great Schism (Rome/Avignon)
the Medici family
Machiavelli

3. To an extent, every era of history is a "time of transition," but that phrase is particularly appropriate to this chapter. The first portion describes the decline of the medieval world, which becomes increasingly morbid and moribund under the influence of plague and war. The last portion begins to describe the glories of the Renaissance, with some excellent cuttings from Machiavelli. Sandwiched between are the rise of the major dynasties of early modern Europe: Valois, Tudor, and Habsburg.

4. The unifying principles are the consolidation of royal power and the rise of a money economy, two elements which were, in practice, often closely linked. Monarchs, with funds at their disposal, could hire administrators, soldiers, and sailors, to increase their power. The administrators, soldiers, and sailors, on the other hand, could provide the stability necessary to protect and increase trade, and the muscle to collect taxes for the monarchs. Some smaller units, like the city-states of the Italy and parts of Germany also made the formula work for relatively short periods, but ultimately it was only the national monarchs who had the power base for success.

5. Study the MAPS on pages 202 (France and England),, 209 (Germany) and Italy (211) and note that though we use twentieth century nation-state names for these areas, none of them really looks much like twentieth century nation-states on the maps.

BOXES

BOX p. 201, "Bias in Place Names" [doing history]. Subtle messages are often sent by the way places are named, and the way these names are spelled and pronounced. This BOX has been expanded for the new edition.

BOX p. 209, "Louis XI" [written record]. This description of the king of France flatters him, not for being glorious and impressive, but for being humble and friendly. Your students might compare the description with Machiavelli's description of a prince on p. 215.

BOX p. 206, "Piers the Plowman" [written record]. Students would do well to remember that this is meant as satire and social criticism. Are there any hints here of the Reformation which will follow in the sixteenth century?

Now let us turn to the specific subheadings of the chapter for consideration of several important details.

I. A WORLD TURNED UPSIDE DOWN

New trends in social history are evident in this introductory essay. Some historians see social history as "history with the political names and dates left out." That is not quite fair, but comparing the number of cited dates and proper nouns in section I (social history) and sections II and III (political history) will demonstrate that such pundits have a point.

The disastrous impact of the Black Death cannot be overestimated. Ask your students to think of how life in their own home town (or their college or university) would change if within a single year about half the people--of all kinds--suddenly died. The importance of gender and class are also stressed in this section; note especially the relatively attractive life style of women of the leisure classes, though in terms of day to day grimy work the men and the women of the lowest class were probably more equal to each other.

TO DEFINE AND DISCUSS:
the great famine of 1315-1317
neofeudal
the four humors
medieval medical care

II. THE EMERGING NATIONAL MONARCHIES

The Hundred Years' War, 1337-1453, is closely related to the struggles between the French and English rulers going back to the Norman conquest of 1066. In a sense, it is part of a rivalry and on-and-off warfare extending up to the Napoleonic Wars. Thus the "100 Years" was only part of nearly 800 years of struggle. But in addition to being a struggle between neighboring monarchs it was--and this is perhaps more important in the long run--part of a struggle of each dynasty to consolidate its power within its own land. This is particularly true for the kings of France, which is clear from a glance at the MAP for page 202, but also for the English, when one remembers that the French supported Scottish and Irish struggles against rule from London.

The conquest of Spain for the Christian monarchies of Ferdinand and Isabella, culminating in the banner year 1492, was alluded to in the previous discussion of the Crusades. But it bears special notice here because it fits in well with the theme of national monarchies. Not to be forgotten, however, is that the reconquest led to the forceful imposition of Catholic orthodoxy on Muslims and Jews who made up a large and productive portion of the Iberian population.

You and the students may wish to spend some time with the GENEALOGICAL CHART on page 206 illustrating the family relationships between the Lancastrians and Yorkists (the red and white roses, respectively). Some students love such charts, and it is possible to get bogged down trying to describe just what the family relationship was between competing branches of some dynastic quarrel. The point should be, I think, to show how in a monarchical age, family struggles were of massive political importance.

TO DEFINE, LOCATE, AND DISCUSS:
Flanders
Calais
apanages
Armagnac
Burgundy
the *taille*
John Wycliffe and the Lollards
House of Commons and House of Lords
Robin Hood
Richard III
Aragon and Castille
the Inquisition
Marranos

III. PARTICULARISM IN GERMANY AND ITALY

While the French and English kings were struggling with some success to centralize their realms, the Holy Roman emperor was having no luck in centralizing his sprawling domain, and in Italy there was not even a monarch in a position from which he could try to create an Italian national state. Indeed, the very fact the overlord of the German and Italian states was THE EMPEROR who had pretensions to world-wide power, meant that there was really no one with the motivation to create an national monarchy in either region.

Early in the twentieth century, before the abysmal destruction of the two "World Wars," historians and political philosophers believed (or assumed) that nationalism was a supreme good, and lamented the lack of national unity in medieval Central Europe. As we approach the end of the twentieth century, and especially having seen the dangers of nationalism run wild in Italy and even more in Germany, many of us are less sure that national self determination is a good end in itself, and thus we are more tolerant of the richly diverse particularlistic states of the "the Germanies" and the Italian peninsula.

The Hansa cities, the Swiss confederation, and cities to the south like Florence, Venice, and Milan, demonstrated the virtues of bourgeois republicanism. Despots sometimes ruled, chaotic plots were hatched, and philosophers like Machiavelli longed for an end to the divisions which weakened these many small states in comparison to the new national monarchies. But much of the glory we call the Renaissance grew in the fertile soil of these small states, and the fact that no single power could dominate them all made for a plurality of options which invigorated both political and cultural life.

TO DEFINE AND DISCUSS:
The Golden Bull of 1356
pro-papal Guelfs and pro-imperial Ghibellines (see Investiture conflict, page 143)

the Conciliar movement and the papacy
Jan Hus
Milan's *parlamento*
Ludovico Il Moro of Milan
the guilds
Florentine bankers
the *doge* of Venice
Italy as the "school of Europe"

SUMMATION

Two dates, 1453 and 1492, turn up again and again this part of the book, and they are worth noting. Students say they hate memorizing dates, but actually they like to have a FEW GOOD DATES as sign posts to guide them through the long centuries of a civilization course. 1453 is suggested by the authors as a good date for the turning point from medieval to modern, though they hasten to point out that the whole era was one of transition. In the East, Constantinople fell in 1453 to the Turks, ending once and for all the "Roman Empire" if such it could still be called. Greek scholars fled to the West, stimulating the Renaissance. In the West, 1453 is the generally accepted date for the end of the Hundred Years' War, though fighting between the major participants continued in various forms. 1492 is familiar to your students for its importance to the New World, and that is proper. But it was also the date of the end of the long battle to conquer (or reconquer) Spain from the Muslims, and the date of the expulsion of Jews from the Spanish realm, spreading Mediterranean Jewry throughout Western Europe.

CRITICAL THINKING

Whether all this adds up to the "rise of the nation" as the title of the chapter suggests might be debated, but it certainly signified the end of the medieval era and the beginning of something The authors never define the words "nation" or "national" in this chapter, but the uses they make of the terms seem so natural, that one could hardly object. Popular nationalism, it is often argued, does not arise as a major force till the French Revolution of 1789. But there are surely elements of nationalism in the behavior of the English and the French, and in the writings of Machiavelli. The medieval world was being turned upside down by the crises of the fourteenth century, but it was not yet clear what would replace the medieval synthesis. Such questions can be addressed by the students in the CRITICAL THINKING QUESTIONS and in the essay items in the TEST ITEM FILE.

11. THE RENAISSANCE

The MAJOR GOAL of this chapter is to familiarize the students with the culture of the Renaissance, particularly as it appeared in Italy. The chapter concentrates on cultural manifestations of the Renaissance, reducing political history to the absolute minimum. If you have not spent enough time on the final section of Chapter 10, therefore, you may wish to double back a bit to provide the political setting for this cultural flowering.

The NINTH EDITION is slightly abridged from the previous editions, and some of the boxes and illustrations have been deleted. The overall structure and concept is unchanged. Blacks in Renaissance Italy are introduced in a new paragraph. There are subtle changes in the treatment of women's history.

BASIC OBJECTIVES

1. The chapter headings contain no obscure or specialized terminology, but the concept of the word <u>Renaissance</u> is discussed at length and the students would do well to spend some time considering its several meanings.

2. The chapter does contain references to terms and persons which ought to become very familiar to the students. Several of these are well illustrated in color visuals.

Carolingian Renaissance
Renaissance of the Twelfth Century
Hansa
galleys, caravels and galleons
ciompi
put-out system
Lombard bankers
enclosures
bourgeoisie
vernacular
humanitas
Dante Aligheri
Petrarch
Boccaccio
Lorenzo Valla
Erasmus of Rotterdam
Rabelais
Leonardo da Vinci
Gutenberg and movable type

Vesalius
Copernicus
Palestrina
Sandro Botticelli
Michelangelo Buonarotti
Peter Breughel
Albrecht Dürer
Benvenuto Cellini
Castiglione

3. Reducing the Renaissance to a list of "greats" is as ridiculous as reducing chemistry to the periodic table. Somehow you must reach the students to inject them into the lively world and creative maelstrom which was the Renaissance. The BOXES should help here, particularly if you drop back to the BOX in Chapter 10 on Machiavelli for starters. Then leap to the Cellini BOX and flip to the photo of Perseus holding the head of Medusa. (You may wish to refresh your own memory of mythology here.)

4. The link between the Renaissance and the classics should be made very clear to the students, and this gives you a chance to do a bit of reviewing of Chapters 2 and 3 as well. Note for example, the statue on page 52 of "the Capitoline wolf" to which the figures of Romulus and Remus were added during the Renaissance. Or have them check Chapter 1 for references to the Biblical David and then consider Michaelangelo's statue.

5. Recently something called "secular humanism" by its critics has been denounced in some quarters, and attempts have been made to ban it from the classrooms of the pure in heart. Fortunately such efforts have not penetrated to this book. But you may get a good discussion going among your students about the relationship between religion, the secular world, the Renaissance, and "humanism." Surely secularism was on the rise during the Renaissance, but Christian humanism as represented by Erasmus was vitally important. And nearly all of Michaelangelo's greatest works were religious in theme.

BOXES

BOX p. 228, "Renaissance Satire" [written record]. The earthy references to foods may appeal to the sense of humor of your students. But try to engage them to debate when does an egg become a chicken. Here is a potentially serious issue!

BOX p. 233, "The Artist's Life" [written record]. With a new title and improved introduction, this selection provides intimate insights into the joys and sorrows of a Renaissance man. A photo of the statue in question is on the facing page, p. 232. Does the son of Zeus resemble the son of a prostitute?

BOX p. 235. "The Courtier" [closer look, which also fits the category written record]. Castiglione's frank permissiveness toward sensual love may inform your students that sexual activity was not invented by their generation.

Now let us turn to the specific subheadings of the chapter for consideration of several important details.

I. A MONEY ECONOMY

Students may perhaps say: "So what! All economies deal with money." But, of course, you have already shown them that the use of cash nearly died out during the early middle ages, and significant amounts of coinage was still rare for the great majority of people during the Renaissance period. Moreover, a money economy meant that trade could be carried out by fund transfers through bills of exchange and other commercial maneuvers as well. Students should be cautioned that this does not yet mean the "industrial revolution" that they have been eagerly awaiting. But that important word BOURGEOISIE is beginning to appear more frequently.

TO DEFINE, LOCATE, AND DISCUSS

Flanders
Lübeck
Florence
Venice
growth of capitalism
arsenalotti
florins
Fugger family of Augsburg
Jacques Coeur
end of serfdom

II. PRINTING, THOUGHT, AND LITERATURE
&
III. SCIENCE AND RELIGION

The Janus face of the Renaissance is well demonstrated by the intellectual history of the time. The rebirth of interest in classical antiquity demanded the mastery of ancient Greek and Latin, languages long "dead" in Western Europe; but the delight in literature and the literary traditions of the classics spurred the creativity which manifested itself in the new vernacular literature, such as Dante's *Divine Comedy*. Similarly in science, humanists revered the work of the classic Galen, but the questioning minds of Renaissance scholars like Vesalius eventually overturned his simplistic ideas. In both fields the new craft of printing made possible systematic communication of the new scholarship.

TO DEFINE AND DISCUSS

the *langue d'oc* and the *langue d'oïl*
Cicero's *studias humanitas*
the sonnet
Donation of Constantine

Pico della Mirandola
Carnival and Lent
geocentric and heliocentric
Giovanni Palestrina

VI. THE FINE ARTS
&
V. THE ART OF DAILY LIVING

It is such a temptation to lapse into (or rise to) a history-of-art lecture when once comes to the Renaissance, and indeed perhaps the temptation should not be resisted. Get out the slide projector, make transparencies for the overhead projector, or get some large prints of the great paintings presented so skillfully in miniature in the textbook. Will your students be shocked by the open displays of sensuality in Botticelli or Michelangelo? Perhaps they should be. Many Renaissance people were. Savonarola comes up in the next chapter. In spite of the substantial use of visuals in this edition, Renaissance architecture comes up rather short in this chapter, but you can have your students turn ahead to the next one to get an idea of the glory of St. Peter's in Rome. We must not ignore the importance of daily life; recall that the "rebirth" of culture did not benefit all people equally. Recent scholars have suggested that women gained little from the Renaissance. Erasmus once wrote that even the "lowliest woman" should read the Bible for herself! He was a master of irony; was he using irony here?

TO DEFINE AND DISCUSS

The Birth of Venus
Masaccio
chiaroscuro
The Last Supper
Cellini's autobiography
Donatello
Pieta
palazzo
the "universal man"
the courtier

SUMMATION

Pause to think a moment about the lifespan of Michelangelo Buonarotti, 1475-1564. In that ninety years the world changed immensely. Another chapter will deal with the geographical explorations of that period, and yet another will deal with the breakup of the medieval church. Copernicus conceived of a new universe, and many a king and prince rose and fell, giving Machiavelli examples with which to populate his commentaries. At some time or another you have probably seen the film version of "The Agony and the Ecstasy," and you may find an ally in Hollywood to bring some life to the Renaissance for your more recalcitrant students. Do not despair. If Michelangelo had had Hollywood's technology at hand do you think he would not have made at least one film? He tried all the other arts, and with success. What kind of a film would he have made?

CRITICAL THINKING

If it is true that death and rebirth are a recurring cycle, how does this one period deserve the name THE Renaissance? The concept was partly an invention of nineteenth-century historians, partly a concept of the Renaissance (and women) themselves. There are plenty of questions here for discussion and for essay writing, and we will return to them in the Test Item File.

12. THE PROTESTANT REFORMATION

The MAJOR GOAL of this chapter is to familiarize the students with the great religious turning points we know as the Protestant and the Catholic Reformations. The emphasis is on the Protestants, because they initiated the change. But Catholic Reform is addressed as well. Some commentators may object that introductory texts giving short shrift to religion, but certainly that is not the case with this book.

The NINTH EDITION the chapter by deleting details here and there throughout the chapter, but the overall structure and interpretation remains the same. Some of the deletions are commentary, such as the final sentence of the chapter from the eighth edition: "The study of the Reformation is a superb example of the growing emphasis in history on the incredibly complex interconnectedness of all human activities."

BASIC OBJECTIVES

1. Every student should recognize and attempt to grasp the significance of the major reformers, both Protestant and Catholic, and the nature of the reform for which each stood.

Martin Luther
Zwingli and Calvin
Henry VIII
the Anabaptists
predestination
Ignatius Loyola
the Jesuits
the Inquisition
the Council of Trent

2. All the students should demonstrate an understanding of the other major events, persons, and concepts in the chapter.

Protestant and Reformed
Anglican
justification by faith vs. by good works
Scholasticism
Savonarola
indulgences
the 95 Theses
Charles V
cuius regio, eius religio
the Peasants' Rebellion
transubstantiation
consubstantiation

John Knox
Huguenot
Mennonites
the *Index*
the "Protestant ethic"

3. Your students, probably, will come from a variety of religious backgrounds, and they will approach religion with attitudes ranging from committed belief to indifference or perhaps even scorn. Some may therefore take offense that their particular point of view is not "properly" represented in the text. Here is the chance to make the American ideal of religious tolerance and pluralism a reality. Yet it should be done with care so that all religious controversy is not eliminated, leaving this exciting era bland and meaningless.

4. Students may benefit from being reminded that the religious groups of today are not the same as those of the sixteenth century, even though they may be descended from them and even bear the same names. You may wish to start with a simple chart:

Roman Catholic = Roman Catholic
Lutheran   = Lutheran
Calvinist   = Reformed, Puritan, Presbyterian
Anglican   = Episcopalian
Anabaptist   = Mennonite, German Baptist, Amish

But then remind them that beliefs and practices have changed dramatically in the last 400 years. Predestination, for example, is no longer an article of faith for the Presbyterians, and indulgences no longer play a major role in Catholic practice. Moreover, a great number of religious groups popular today (like Methodists and American Baptists) were not established during the Reformation, but later split off from the sixteenth century Protestant organizations.

5. This chapter is purged of all but the most essential political material, because that aspect of the period is dealt with in the following chapter, THE GREAT POWERS IN CONFLICT. If you are moving rapidly through this textbook you may wish to assign chapters 12 and 13 together.

BOXES

BOX p. 240 "Luther on Christian Liberty" [written record]. This BOX is shorter than in the eighth edition because section from *To the Christian Nobility of the German Nation* has been cut. The emphasis here is now clearly on the question of human freedom, free will, and its political and social implications. You might point out the implications for Luther's political conservatism and his reaction to the Peasants' Rebellion.

BOX p. 249 "The Inquisition" [written record]. At first blush the Inquisition does not looks particularly oppressive in this example. But students may get the drift when the subtlety of the argument is pointed out and compared with the print of executions on the facing page.

Now let us turn to the specific subheadings of the chapter for consideration of several important details.

I. PROTESTANT FOUNDERS: MARTIN LUTHER
&
II. ZWINGLI, CALVIN, AND OTHER FOUNDERS
&
III. PROTESTANT BELIEFS AND PRACTICES

The story of the dedicated German monk who struggled with his own faith and ended up by shaping the faith of millions is an excellent narrative, which should not be missed in your rush to the modern age. Roland Bainton's sympathetic biography is cited in the bibliography and filled with useful material for your lectures or your students' term papers. Other great figures of the era can be added for contrast, fairness and balance, if you wish, like Erasmus or Loyola.

A biographical approach is useful here lest you and your students get bogged down in theologizing. Some theology is necessary to realize the distinction between salvation by <u>faith alone</u> and salvation through <u>good works</u>. But I believe that only through personalizing the issues can your students get an appreciation of the *Angst* (fear and trembling) which Luther felt when he faced the problem of his own sinfulness. The leaders of the Reformation were genuinely worried about their own eternal salvation (or perdition).

The chapter tends to understate the political aspects of the Reformation, except for the break of Henry with Rome. Quite correctly the authors avoid the use of the word <u>divorce</u> when discussing that event; if your students wish to trace the British royals, see the next chapter for the family tree. The whole political context of the Reformation is described there.

TO DEFINE AND DISCUSS

"priesthood of all believers,"
the Diet at Worms
Luther's conservatism
Switzerland
"free will"
Catherine of Aragon
antinomian anarchism
Michael Servetus
Erastianism
Arminianism

IV. THE CATHOLIC REFORMATION

A generation ago this movement was called the "Counter Reformation," because it was believed to be no more than a reaction to the Protestant challenge. Much of the traditional Anglo-American historiography of the Reformation has had a distinctively anti-Catholic slant; the print of the people being burned by the Inquisition gives you a taste of that approach. That type of propaganda has fortunately been edited out of this book (we do not even have a mention of Queen "Bloody" Mary here, though she makes it into the next chapter). The rigor and the virtue of the Society of Jesus and the Trentine church is quite properly emphasized, while it is made clear that in the sixteenth century neither Catholic nor Protestant believed in our own ideals of religious pluralism and toleration. The next chapter recounts the wars of religion, and you may wish to have your students glance ahead a bit so that they will realize that the claiming of souls for the church was not entirely a peaceful process.

TO DEFINE, LOCATE, AND DISCUSS

Loyola's *Spiritual Exercises*
Trent
seven sacraments

V. PROTESTANTISM AND THE IDEA OF PROGRESS
&
SUMMATION

The interpretive essay ending this chapter can be used in several ways. If your students are relatively unsophisticated, or if you are especially pressed for time, you may omit it from the reading assignments and use it yourself for lecture material. If your students like to discuss, and you have the time and the class size to permit it, you might arrange a debate on the question WHAT WAS MODERN IN THE PROTESTANT REFORMATION? It would probably be a lively class period. If you have a very well prepared group of students, you may help them to see why much to the historiography of today's scholars has moved beyond that debate. To do this you might wish to turn to work by Steven Ozment and Natalie Davis, which employ the "new" social history to get beyond the theological and political rhetoric into the lives of the common people. You could even show the them parts of the film "The Return of Martin Guerre." But whatever you do, you should be sure your students are aware of the ideal of "the Protestant ethic," because (be they Protestant or not) they may need a good deal of that ethic to do well in your course.

CRITICAL THINKING

Counterfactual history is sometimes useful as a stimulus to historical thinking. What would have happened, you might ask your students, if Henry VIII had had a healthy son by Catherine of Aragon and felt no need for an annulment? What if Luther had followed his original career plans become a wealthy and satisfied lawyer rather than a rebellious monk? Would there have still been a reformation of medieval Catholicism? Would our world have become "modern" sooner or later anyway?

13. THE GREAT POWERS IN CONFLICT

The MAJOR GOAL of this chapter is to familiarize the students with the political and diplomatic struggles of the sixteenth and seventeenth centuries. But there are two sub-plots as well which are very important in the total picture of world history, indeed perhaps even more important than the details of the political and diplomatic narrative. The first is the concept of *long durée* in social and economic history. The second is the scientific revolution.

The NINTH EDITION of this chapter is an abrieviated version of the previous edition, with many details and some interpretive comments deleted. The concept and the structure is unchanged.

BASIC OBJECTIVES

1. The students should have a strong understanding of the major concepts and events mentioned in the chapter's headings and subheadings.

long durée
the Dutch revolt
absolutism
the Peace of Westphalia
the scientific revolution

2. The students should understand the other basic concepts, major events, and geographical terms in the chapter.

balance of power
hegemony
republic
nation-state
international law
Valois dynasty
Bourbon dynasty
Habsburg dynasty
Tudor dynasty
the house of Orange
elector of the Holy Roman Empire
Palatinate
Bohemia
rationalism
cogito ergo sum

3. The details of the kings, wars, battles, and treaties, will probably be a bit bewildering for your students. The Habsburg-Valois Wars and

the Thirty Years' War are remarkable in their complexity, and perhaps you will not have the time to narrate and analyze them in the detail which they deserve. The key point around which to organize all this bloodshed, probably, is the idea of the "balance of power." The various dynasties each attempt to gain <u>hegemony</u> over the states of Europe, but each was eventually checked by a coalition of the other powers, great and small.

4. The chapter makes much of the concept of "modernity," as well it should. If you have been using this book in its <u>two volume</u> to teach the ancient and medieval worlds, you are now coming toward the end of the first volume, and you would do well to point out to them how the world has changed since the first chapters. This is easiest with the scientific and technological aspects of history, but it can be done with the geographical and political as well, because the MAP of Europe is beginning to look rather familiar, at least in the areas which touch the Atlantic.

BOXES

BOX p. 264 *Don Quixote* [written record]. Point out the irony in the selection, noting that the unlettered Sancho apparently knows how to take care of himself better than the aristocratic Don Quixote. You probably should mention that many Americans now know these figures through the distorted lens of the Broadway musical. You might also comment on the two variant pronuciations, kee-HOH-tay closer to the Spanish original, and KWICK-ot used by our British cousins and appearing in our word *quixotic*.

BOX p. 267 The Edict of Nantes [written record]. Link this document with the concept of the *politiques* on the same page. Perhaps you should flash forward also to let the students know that this "perpetual and irrevocable" edict was revoked by Louis XIV less than a century later.

BOX p. 270 The English Aristocracy [closer look]. This important piece of social analysis appeared as part of the general text in the former edition. The author highlights it here because of its importance.

QUESTIONS FOR DISCUSSION

1. Describe the power struggle between the great dynastic monarchies (which are becoming nation-states) during the sixteenth and early seventeenth century. What was the role of Spain and the New World? Of England and the Dutch? Of France and the Italian states? Of the German and Scandinavian states?

2. How did the nature of warfare change during the shift from the medieval to the modern world? What new weapons were being used [see the PICTURES]? What was the role of religious ideology? What was the role of national patriotism? What were the roles of the traditional nobility and the common soldiers? What was the importance of money, as opposed to feudal obligations?

3. What were the social and economic underpinnings of the political and diplomatic events of this period? How did the "long durée" of population upswing in the sixteenth century, and the disastrous effects of bad harvests and wars in the "crisis of the seventeenth century" affect the lives of the people and the major events of the age?

4. How did the ideas of Copernicus, Galileo, Descartes, Newton, and others challenge the traditional ideas and ideals of knowledge? What place did God have in a universe which seemed so rational? And what place did the church (Protestant or Catholic) have in a world so dominated by openly secular struggles for wealth and power? In what ways was the modern age that was dawning in the sixteenth and century better than the medieval world, and in what ways was it worse?

Note that this question openly calls for value judgments by the students. Those who see the study of history as a value-free science may object to this question. I would suggest that in doing so they are setting up some pretty powerful values of their own.

Now let us turn to the specific subheadings of the chapter for consideration of several important details.

I. A LONG DUREE

The two essays which begin this chapter raise important, if somewhat abstract-sounding, points of historical interpretation for the students. Reflecting the newest of scholarship, they show by example that history is not merely "one damn thing after another." (There are plenty of "facts" packed elsewhere into the chapter.) I sometimes ask my students "when did the modern age start?" Often they say that it is the twentieth century, or even perhaps that real modernity did not start till they were born. This chapter starts with the answers to that question that historians give, and your students should be aware of the concept of "modern" which our discipline has developed.

The "long sixteenth century" emphasizes the social and economic aspects of the question of modernity, and like all broad generalizations it has to be modified in many specific cases. But it is true that European civilization was coming out of the stagnation of the late middle ages and beginning to assert its position of would-be dominance in the world (as will be shown clearly in the following chapter).

TO DEFINE AND DISCUSS

sovereign states
Pax Britannica
mercenaries
the pike and arquebus
bill of exchange
joint stock company
maritime regulations

II. A COMPLEXITY OF WARS
&
III. THE CATHOLIC MONARCHIES: SPAIN AND FRANCE

The attempts of the Habsburg dynasty to gain hegemony form the theme around which one can organize the the many monarchs and their battles and treaties which fill this part of the chapter. It was the French monarchs who first marched into Italy, using the power of a nation-based dynasty against the disunited city-states of the Italian peninsula. But the Valois French soon came into direct confrontation with the Spanish Habsburgs, and they were unable to dominate Italy. The Spanish Habsburgs, on the other hand, tried to keep control of the Low Countries on the other northern flank of the French monarchy and found themselves facing coalitions of Valois French and Tudor English, as well as the Dutch Protestant Republic. The French Valois dissipated much of their energy in religious warfare, and the dynasty finally succumbed to the related dynasty of the Bourbons, which attempted to stabilize the French monarchy through toleration.

In all this gore the great accomplishments of Spanish culture during the period are highlighted, as in the BOX on Don Quixote and Sancho Panza, and the color reproductions of El Greco.

TO DEFINE AND DISCUSS

Francis I (Valois)
Charles V (Habsburg)
Philip II (Habsburg)
the Escorial palace/monastery
the Cortes
mercantilism
anti-Semitism
Cervantes
the *parlements* in France
Huguenots
Catherine de' Medici
Henry IV (Bourbon)
the Edict of Nantes

IV. THE PROTESTANT STATES:
TUDOR ENGLAND AND THE DUTCH REPUBLIC
&
V. GERMANY AND THE THIRTY YEARS' WAR

It is useful to divide the monarchies between Catholic and Protestant as the authors have done, but one should not assume that all the Latin countries were purely Catholic and all the Germanic ones purely Protestant. Religion remained an issue in every major country during the sixteenth century, and surely it was THE MAJOR ISSUE in diplomacy and war through 1648, though it was by no means the only one.

The dominant tradition of American historiography until recently, and continuing in some quarters, is one which emphasizes England and its Protestant allies on the continent. Elizabethan England is of both political and cultural significance, and the inability of the German Habsburgs to establish their domination--religious and political--in the Germanies set the stage for Bismarck's unification of Germany in the nineteenth century, a unification so recently achieved again.

Yet these two sections point up one of the most significant points in the period: religion may still be used as the ideological excuse for battle, but secular aims are increasingly important, and even openly espoused. Note the role of the French minister Richelieu during the Thirty Years' War, a Cardinal of the Roman Catholic Church sponsoring the Protestants in the German wars because it was in the interest of his country, France, to do so.

TO DEFINE AND DISCUSS

Henry VIII (Tudor) and his first wife, Catherine of Aragon, and second wife, Anne Boleyn
gentry class
"Bloody" Mary (Tudor) and her husband Philip of Spain (Habsburg)
Elizabeth I and the Elizabethan age
the English Renaissance
the Dutch Republic
Spinoza
the Peace of Augsburg (1555)
Ferdinand (Habsburg)
Frederick V of the Palatinate
Christian IV of Denmark
Maximilian of Bavaria
Gustavus Adolphus of Sweden
Jacques Callot on the *Miseries of War*
the Peace of Westphalia (1648) and the Treaty of the Pyrenees (1659)

VI. SCIENCE AND RELIGION

Some textbooks devote an entire chapter to the scientific revolution, while this one puts that major turning point in the intellectual history of the world at the end of a chapter on great power politics. You may wish to treat this section as a chapter in and of itself, linking it to Part III of Chapter 11 [Science and Religion in the Renaissance] and to Chapter 17 [The Enlightenment]. If you are confident that your studentds are getting adquate understanding from their science classes,you may chose to bypass it with only a glance.

The greatest danger in handling the topic is in giving the students the simplified idea that the geniuses of the seventeenth century overturned the wrong-headed and superstitious beliefs of the ancient and medieval world and discovered perfect truth. As a matter of fact, certain aspects of the medieval synthesis made good common sense, given the circumstances of the time, while some of the breakthroughs of the scientific revolution have been far surpassed by the new scientific theories of the twentieth century. For example, Copernicus suggested that the sun was the center of the universe and all the planets moved in circular orbits; no astronomer would hold that today.

One important concept for your students is the distinction between inductive and deductive reasoning. The inductive (or empirical) approach emphasizes the collection of information, from which a generalization is then drawn. The deductive method moves logically from basic assumptions to appropriate conclusions (as in geometry). The scientific revolution did not throw out deductive reasoning in favor of an inductive approach; it used both kinds of reasoning to check each other. Newton's *Principia* is largely a deductive (mathematical) work, but used the data inductively compiled by others to arrive at its conclusions.

TO DEFINE AND DISCUSS

Francis Bacon
Blaise Pascal
Robert Boyle
Sir Isaac Newton
William Harvey
René Descartes
Galileo.

SUMMATION

During the seventeenth century the great monarchies of Western Europe not only asserted themselves politically, diplomatically, and militarily. They also began to support the developments in the sciences which they believed would ultimately provide their countries wealth and power. When the United States government put money into a space-based defense system, therefore, it was following in the tradition of the monarchs of this period. Some of the monarchs no doubt thought themselves merely continuing the ideal of Renaissance patronage of artists and scholars, but the importance of the new science and technology for the practical crafts of commerce and war soon showed them otherwise. Thus it makes some sense to include the scientific revolution in a chapter on the Great Powers in Conflict, just as it would make sense to see the development of space technology in the second half of the twentieth century as part of the U.S.-Soviet Cold War.

CRITICAL THINKING

Military and diplomatic history is sometimes rejected by our new generation of historians as unworthy of emphasis in our classes today. The "war and society" approach, however, makes a lot of sense. Help your students think of the importance of military power in "the Spanish century" and in the brutal chaos of the Thirty Years' War. Some commentators have suggested similarities between that bloody struggle and the two world wars of the first half of the twentieth century.

14. EXPLORATION AND EXPANSION

The MAJOR GOAL of this chapter is to familiarize the students with the overseas voyages of Europeans between the late 15th and the late 18th centuries, and the impact which those voyages and the colonialism accompanying them had on both the European and the non-European societies. Thus the chronological and the geographical scope of this chapter is very broad, probably the broadest of the book.

The NINTH EDITION shortens the chapter by cutting some of the commentary, but it maintains some of the material critical of Columbus and of European civilization in general which was added in the eighth edition. The general outlines and coverage remain the same.

BASIC OBJECTIVES

1. The chapter headings and subheadings are filled with geographical names, and all your students should be able to locate them all on a blank map of the world. Reference to some of these areas seem so elementary that it is embarrassing to even to raise the issue with a college class. But you may be unhappily surprised. Try passing out a blank world map (or even just a blank sheet of paper) and asking your students to free hand draw a map of the world locating all of the following:

Portugal
Africa
India
China
Spain
England
the Netherlands (home of the Dutch)
Sweden
France
the East Indies
the West Indies
Russia
the Far East

2. Students should also be able to locate, in both _time_ and _space_, the following important places and people from the chapter.

Viking voyages to North America
Prince Henry the Navigator
Marco Polo
Vasco da Gama
Treaty of Tordesillas

medieval Ghana
Timbuktu
Hindu
the caste system of India
Buddhism
Confucius
mercantilism
Columbus
Magellan
Cartier and Champlain
Sir Walter Raleigh
New Amsterdam
the Caribbean
the Dutch East Indies
Siberia
Tokugawa Japan
the slave trade
Captain James Cook

3. The chapter quite rightly points out that the traditional approach to "the known world" is extremely Eurocentric. As a matter of fact, at the beginning of the age of exploration, Europeans were not particularly highly civilized, when compared to the peoples of the non-West. Even long after European explorers and conquerors seemed to have established their dominance, they were merely looked upon as well armed barbarians by many leaders of the non-West.

4. The major question arises, therefore, just why and how the Europeans were so successful in coming to dominate the world for several centuries. Military and naval technology gives us part of the answer, but one must also look to the major trends which have been dealt with in earlier chapters, such as religious zeal, the commercial revolution, and the power of the new monarchies.

5. Questions of race and slavery are important to this chapter, and should be increasingly important in your course, given the current considerations of "multiculturalism." The BOXES and the PICTURES show something of the non-Western world, and its ideals. Try to have your students gain something of a non-white person's view of the "age of exploration" using this material. Though this chapter (and the book as a whole) makes no attempt to give all civilizations "equal time," the authors do try to bring some balance of perspective, so that students will not simply presume European (i.e. white) superiority and fail to ask some important questions about why things happened as they did.

BOXES

BOX p. 291 "Columbus Describes the New World" [written record]. To get the support of the Spanish monarchy for his voyage, Columbus had promised to find a way to East Asia. But rather than the highly literate civilizations of Japan or China, he found the Caribbean islanders living a simple life in lush surroundings. How could Columbus put a positive spin on his failure to find the civilization he had expected and promised? Remind your students that Columbus wanted to convince Ferdinand and Isabella to put up more money to finance his next voyage, even though this one had not paid off in commercial terms.

BOX p. 293 "The Hazards of Exploration" [written record]. Your students should get a good idea of the brutal hardships endured by the sailors of the sixteenth century. If the regular sailors had it this bad, consider how slave cargoes were treated on slave vessels.

BOX p. 297 "A Japanese Folk Tale" [written record]. You might discuss this item by beginning with the question "who was discovering who?"

BOX p. 299 "The Slave Trade" [written record]. There are several levels for reading these two texts. The most important, no doubt, is to use one's imagination to get a sense of the human suffering involved. The color picture on the same page helps in this regard (though it is from a later period). On another level consider the role of the unidentified privateer; one might speculate on who these "rovers" were. Finally, note the importance of profit for the investors involved. The commercial revolution had reduced everything to a balance sheet.

BOX p. 300 "The Importance of Cotton" [closer look, incorporating a section of a primary source document]. You might ask how many of your students are wearing something of cotton, then point out how rare and expensive cotton was in the sixteenth century. Finally, link it to slavery in the Americas

QUESTIONS FOR DISCUSSION

1. Describe the voyages of the major European explorers during the fifteenth and sixteenth centuries. Who were they, and where did they go? More importantly, why did they do it, and what factors contributed to their success?

2. Describe the competition and conflicts among the European great powers as they struggled to dominate the worlds newly discovered, especially North America. How might things be different for Americans today if England had not emerged dominant in the late 18th century? What would have happened if Queen Mary of England and King Philip of Spain, who married in the mid-1500's, had had a son who would have inherited both the crowns and gone on to a long and successful rule? [See previous chapter.]

3. Compare and contrast the responses to European colonization of the two largest countries in Asia, India and China. What circumstances permitted each to respond differently, and how have those differences contributed to the situations in those to countries today?

Now let us turn to the specific subheadings of the chapter for consideration of several important details.

I. EXPLORATION AND EXPANSION
&
V. THE IMPACT OF EXPANSION

The first and last sections of this chapter raise important theoretical and conceptual questions about the traditional approach to the subject at hand. On the whole, Europeans (and their descendants throughout the world) have assumed the superiority of their culture, and they have seen the expansion of it into the wider world as a great favor to the non-Western peoples. To be sure, the more brutal and exploitive aspects of imperialism have not been ignored or justified; indeed, Westerners have vied with one another to show how the expansion of one or another of their empires or ideologies would save the non-Westerners from abominable evils. The British justified their rule as particularly enlightened in the nineteenth century. During the Cold War, the Soviet Union supported costly "wars of national liberation" to bring the glory of communism to the non-West.

With the perspective of the late twentieth century, however, we can see that the age of exploration and expansion brought with it complex and many-sided challenges and responses. West and non-West interacted in many ways. Note, for example the question of the Africans who were forcibly settled in the Americas. Slavery was an old institution among Africans, but it changed dramatically because of the white slave traders. Blacks eventually achieved liberty in the Americas and have contributed mightily to Western civilization as it exists today. African nations are now independent of their former colonial masters; they have endured exploitation, but gained much from the experience.

TO DEFINE AND DISCUSS

revolution of rising expectations
tobacco
maize
tea and coffee
missionary zeal
the medieval "cake of custom"

II. EAST BY SEA TO THE INDIES
&
III. WEST BY SEA TO THE INDIES
&
IV. THE NORTH ATLANTIC POWERS

During the late fifteenth century Portugal and Spain were the chief contenders for the world wide balance of power, but before the sixteenth century was over, the northern powers of England, France, and the Dutch rose to dominance. It was not until after 1945 that these powers lost their control over areas vast distances from the "mother countries."

Be sure to make full use of the MAP TRANSPARENCY for this chapter, because you simply cannot assume that your students have the geographical vocabulary to understand what was going on. You should also make use of the time line chart on pp. 304 and 305. Indeed, and interesting assignment would be to add another strip along it entitled "the non-European world."

TO DEFINE, LOCATE, AND DISCUSS

Dias
Afonso de Albuquerque
Goa
Zimbabwe
Mogul (Mughal, Mongol) empire
Brahmins
nirvana
the Manchus
factors and factory
the *Lusiads* of Liuz de Camoes
Cipangu
Amerigo Vespucci
the Northwest Passage
Cortes and Pizarro
Creoles and mestizos
Las Casas
Verrazzano
Fort Christina
Quebec and Louisiana
the Dutch at the Cape of Good Hope
Japanese isolation

V. RUSSIA

It is important to remember that exploration can be by land as well as by sea. Americans, with their ideal of Manifest Destiny, should have a good feel for this once they have been reminded. In this case, it is the expansion of European Russia into Asia which is the case in point. We would do well to realize that Russian expansion began in the same period as the Western European expansion across the Atlantic.

TO DEFINE, LOCATE, AND DISCUSS

Ivan the Terrible
the Ural mountains
Okhotsk
the Amur valley
Vitus Bering

SUMMATION

When we observed the quincenntenial of Columbus's voyage to the America in 1992, there was much talk about the meaning of his achievements.

Some of the activities were merely boosterism and commercial propaganda. Some had a political agenda, more or less specific. Some of the activities had genuine historical content. You may still be able to make use of a great deal of this material for teaching purposes. We Americans have been the beneficiaries of a great many peoples of varying traditions. If we can welcome and make use of this pluralism, rather than allowing it to become a point of continuing and pointless conflict, we will continue to benefit on even a higher level.

CRITICAL THINKING

Our ideas of travel and communication have shrunken the world so much, that it is hard to imagine what voyages meant in the early modern period. Use MAPS to emphasize distance and time for ships under sail, or for people walking or riding horses. Without romanticizing the achievements of the Europeans, and without ignoring the brutalities of exploration and conquest, try to bring your students of every race and heritage to understand the extraordinary changes which the age of exploration created. Essay assignments, or essay questions on exams, can give them freedom to express themselves on these changes.

15. The Problem of Divine Right Monarchy

The MAJOR GOAL of Chapter 15 is to compare and contrast the state-building of seventeenth century Bourbon France with that of Stuart England. In each country a vigorous dynasty tried to impose a "modern" absolute monarchy upon a relatively chaotic early modern political structure. The Bourbons were successful, creating a reasonably centralized state justified with the doctrine of divine right. The Stuarts failed, losing the throne for a generation in a revolutionary upheaval and regaining it only by compromising on a constitution with the forces of parliament. This contrast is reflected in the dichotomies of the final section of the chapter, gentleman/everyman and progress/pessimism.

The NINTH EDITION is little changed from the eighth edition, which had provided some modification of earlier editions on the material on witchcraft.

BASIC OBJECTIVES

1. The student should analyze what the authors mean by the major terms used in the chapter's title and sub-headings:

divine-right monarchy
English Civil War, Revolution, and Interregnum
the Glorious Revolution
Baroque

2. The student should recognize and be able to identify or define the key individuals, places and event treated in the chapter.

raison d'état
parlement
asiento
Fronde
Gallican Church
Jansenism
mercantilism
Puritan
millenarians
Whigs and Tories
pretender
Cardinal Richelieu
Oliver Cromwell
John Milton
William Blackstone
Blaise Pascal
Thomas Hobbes

3. In broad terms, but with some command of illustrative details, students should understand the differences between the absolutist divine-right monarchy of the seventeenth century and the medieval monarchies of earlier years.

4. Students should see the importance of ideals of liberty and democracy as they began to arise in Britain, particularly the concepts of the division of powers between crown and parliament. Students must always be reminded that hardly anyone in seventeenth century England was fighting for "democracy" as we know it, but that their efforts formed the foundation for the constitutional democracies of today.

5. Students should consider the role of force in the building of the modern state, and how people can try to limit it when it becomes tyrannical. They should see that law and order under Louis XIV was looked upon with favor by many, because it contrasted dramatically with the brutal chaos of the wars of religion, but that on the other hand Louis XIV used state power equally arbitrarily against the Huguenots with the revocation of the Edict of Nantes. They should see that Cromwell and the Puritans rose against the Stuart attempt to create an absolute monarchy, but that when in power these same men showed little toleration for the liberties of others.

6. The age of the baroque showed a "restless search for power." Students should see the links between the arts, the sciences, and the political struggles of the age. An excellent opportunity for this exercise is provided by the pictures of the major architectural achievements of the era. They also present the opportunity to link the seventeenth century with the classical past, since they use clearly classical vocabulary in new ways.

7. Our students usually have little sympathy for the very idea of divine-right monarchy. Difficult or even absurd as it might seem, they should be given some idea of why it was an ideal which appealed to a great many people in the seventeenth century. The arguments of Thomas Hobbes, though materialist, may be of some use here. Without a centralized authority, life may well prove "nasty, brutish and short." Try assigning one of the brighter students to argue the case for divine-right monarchy against the challenges of students arguing for the rule of the people. The picture of the all-embracing monarch on p. 326 may help get the idea across.

BOXES

BOX p. 310 "*Le grand Monarque*" [written record]. Have the students compare Madame de Motteville's word picture with the painting by Hyacinthe Rigaud on p. 312. Note that the painting is of the older Louis.

BOX p. 321 "Oliver Cromwell" [closer look]. This could also count as an example of the "written record" as well, since it is a primary source document by a famous author, John Milton. Note the praise for

Cromwell's army--it "committed no lawless outrages." Compare that with the descriptions of the depredations of the continental mercenaries of the Thirty Years' War (see p. 274). This is a NEW BOX.

BOX p. 323 "Blackstone on the Law" [written record]. This important commentator, writing a century after the English revolution, highlights the significance of the checks and balances within constitutional government.

BOX p. 327 "Curiosity and Change" [written record]. The descriptive paragraph on Pascal on p. 327 nicely sets up these two paragraphs from his *Pensees*. Pascal demonstrates that there was no sharp distinction between science and religion in the seventeenth century, as perhaps there still is not today.

BOX p. 334 "Who Built the Towers of Thebes?" [written record]. This commentary by a twentieth century German calls for the recognition of the work and the lives of the "little people" who actually raised the stones and baked the bread. You may wish to return to the MAP of Greece on p. 28 to remind your students where Thebes is located (NW of Athens).

QUESTIONS FOR DISCUSSION

1. What combination of forces made Bourbon France so powerful in the seventeenth century?

Note the importance of excellent leadership, centralization of administrative and military strength, and general prosperity based upon security from domestic disorder and international invasion.

2. What combination of forces made Stuart England into a constitutional monarchy by the end of the seventeenth century?

Note the importance of leadership, both excellent and faulty, decentralized administrative and military power, and concepts of law and justice reaching back to Magna Carta and articulated by thinkers like Hobbes and Locke.

3. What was the "problem" of divine-right monarchy?

Note that it was partly a problem of ideas and ideology; partly a problem of weak vs. strong and wise vs. unwise leadership; partly a problem of historical context. Many reasonable people thought that centralized monarchical authority was a good idea, or at least a necessary one, given the chaotic alternatives then available.

Now let us turn to the specific subheadings of the chapter for consideration of several important details.

I. BOURBON FRANCE

The figures of Louis XIII, Cardinal Richelieu, Cardinal Mazarin, and Louis XIV should become familiar to all the students. The textbook links France with Italy by the mention of Machiavellianism. Perhaps someone in the class will recall the Three Musketeers, whose deeds of daring reflect the struggles of the people to avoid the centralizing power of the monarchy.

Those students who have studied some French should now have the opportunity to use their skills in dealing with terms like *raison d'état* and *l'état c'est moi*. The Palace of Versailles can be shown off to students with color slides, photos from books or magazines, or videos and films. Equally important, if a bit less impressive, is the Hotel des Invalides in Paris, the old-soldiers' home and military headquarters, which symbolized the power of the French army. Today's American students often forget that the French were a great military power.

TO DEFINE AND DISCUSS

Colbert and mercantilism
Louvois and the army
Martinet and military discipline
Vauban and fortifications
Balance of power and the War of the Spanish Succession.

II. STUART ENGLAND

Reminding students that the Stuarts were a foreign dynasty (Scottish) will help them to understand one of the reasons why James I and Charles I got into trouble with parliament. The fact that both sides in the religious conflict were Protestant makes the religious issue a bit hard to understand, but reference to the Puritans and the "Pilgrim fathers" as opposed to the elaborate ceremony of high church Anglicanism should help get things clear. The key to the major issue was, of course, the power of the purse strings, which is familiar to many students because of its significance in the American Revolution.

Students may be amazed and amused to find that the word "republican" was considered radical at the time, rather than conservative. The concepts of "Cavalier" and "Roundhead" can be illustrated by the paintings of the time, though even the "Roundheads" still look a bit long-haired by today's standards. Note the paragraph which stresses the importance given to women by some of the more radical groups during the Revolution, p. 322.

With the Stuart Restoration the issue of Catholicism becomes important, and lest the English should seem unnecessarily intolerant the policies of the Catholic Louis XIV should be recalled. Religion was still a major issue in Ireland, as, alas, it still is in the 1990's.

TO DEFINE AND DISCUSS

Ship money
Star Chamber
Ulster
Long Parliament
"Pride's Purge"
New Model Army
Levelers and Diggers
Quakers
the Bill of Rights
the "Old Pretender"

III. CENTURY OF GENIUS/CENTURY OF EVERYMAN

Cultural history sometimes is passed over nearly in silence when one is so busy with political and constitutional questions, but in this case you should especially avoid doing so. The ideas of Hobbes and Locke are directly relevant to the political discussions, and the great baroque buildings, such as Versailles, are as well. Moreover, students are likely to have some passing familiarity with the English literature of the age--Shakespeare to Milton--and some may even be aware of the French masters--Moliere and Pascal. All have at least heard of Rembrandt, and the pictures in the text will give you an opportunity to relate the skills of the artists to the realities of the age. Finally, if you have some musicians in class they may recognize some of the baroque composers, particularly Purcell's trumpet tunes.

Most difficult to discuss, perhaps, but certainly very important, is the ongoing tension between the apparent progress of civilization as a whole and the obvious sufferings of the people. The discussions of witchcraft will help to make this contrast real to the students.

TO DEFINE AND DISCUSS

Spinoza
Dryden
Rubens
Velasquez
Van Dyck
Christopher Wren
Bernini
the plague

SUMMATION

Historians now speak of the "crisis of the seventeenth century," an idea which seems to contrast sharply with the emphasis on positive state and constitution building which most of this chapter has emphasized. The incredible tortures of the Thirty Years' War, which contributed to the "crisis" are treated in Chapter 13. But even the progress in France and England was not bloodless by any means, and common folk suffered substantial hardships. In a survey course it is very difficult to address both the sweep of progress and the bitter defeats along the way.

CRITICAL THINKING

Outlines of constitutional history are readily apparent to all students, but it takes considerable command of detail and critical acumen to relate those outlines to the real events which affected people's lives. Perhaps architecture is a good way to relate the two. The picture of Versailles before it is expanded by Louis (p. 311) is a place to start. If your students have travelled at all, or even if they have not, suggest that they hunt out and bring in graphics of Bourbon chateaux and compare them with the 17th century castles and houses of the Stuarts. Then turn to Brecht's "who built . . ." for some critical thinking exercises.

16. THE OLD REGIMES

The MAJOR GOAL of this chapter is to familiarize the students with the domestic and foreign affairs of the great monarchies (and some of the smaller states) of the 18th century. The concepts of absolutist and constitutional monarchies, the concept of balance of power in foreign affairs, and the socio-economic structure of the Old Regime, are all basic to the chapter.

Often students confuse the balance of power in war and diplomacy with the idea of the separation of powers and checks and balances within constitutional government. In addition, they tend to equate absolute monarchy with 20th century dictatorship and even with totalitarianism. Discussion of historical examples, which abound in the text, in the BOXES and the MAPS should make these distinctions clearer to your students.

The NINETH EDITION is structurally the same as the previous edition, but it has been shortened by deleting some of the details.

BASIC OBJECTIVES

1. The student should analyze what the author means by the terms set forth in the chapter title and the sub-headings, i.e.

Old Regime
agricultural improvements
Industrial Revolution
Prussia and the Hohenzollerns
Peter the Great
the Diplomatic Revolution.

2. The student should recognize and identify (or define) the key individuals, places, and events treated in the chapter, e.g.

mercantilism
cameralism
John Law
Mississippi Bubble
South Sea Bubble
"Turnip" Townshend
domestic system vs. factory system
Robert Walpole
Louis XV
Charles VI
Frederick William I
Elizabeth Farnese
Maria Theresa

As a review, students should be reminded of the names of the major dynasties: Habsburg, Hanoverian, Hohenzollern, Romanov, and Bourbon.

3. Discuss the principles of the balance of power, illustrating the discussion from the material on the 18th century wars, particularly the War of the Austrian Succession and the Seven Years War. The Diplomatic Revolution permits an excellent opportunity to illustrate with the principles of balance of power politics.

4. Discuss the social and economic structure of the Old Regime, noting the differences between lands of western Europe (rise of bourgeoisie) and those of eastern Europe (persistence of serfdom). The COFFEE SHOP and the AGE OF MANNERS inserts (and some of the pictures) will be of great use in this exercise.

5. Compare and contrast the development of constitutional monarchy and parliamentary government in Britain with the development of the absolutist bureaucratic state on the continent, noting that both were superior in terms of state power to the older forms represented by the "victims," Poland and the Ottoman Empire.

6. Though undue present-mindedness should not be encouraged, you may wish to relate the issues and events of the period of the Old Regime to the world of today. For example, are there any monarchies left in the world today? If so, are they a kind of absolutist "old regime" in which we might well find a future revolution? Or are they "constitutional" and moving in the direction of liberalization? Do commercial factors enter into the foreign policies of countries now as then?

BOXES

BOX p. 338 "The Coffeehouse" [closer look]. Students may wish to compare the business day of the eighteenth century to that of today. How much informal business is done over "coffee breaks"?

BOX p. 346 "An Age of Manners" [written record]. Consider how these proprieties are associated with "civilized behavior." Even children need privacy for their natural functions. Note how this code of conduct distinguishes the educated classes from the uncouth peasantry. The BOX has been shortened somewhat from the previous edition.

BOX p. 349 "Peter the Great" [written record]. Note this view of Peter, by a Russian critic, was written at least two generations after his death.

QUESTIONS FOR DISCUSSION

1. Why is this period sometimes called the "age of monarchy"? Describe different kinds of monarchy dealt with in the chapter, giving examples.

Note the differences between medieval (weak) and absolutist (strong) monarchies.

2. What can one imply about the social structure of the Old Regime from the pictures in the text? Compare the woman running the spinning jenny with the luxury of Madame de Pompadour.

3. Sometimes it is said that the balance of power is a system of diplomacy designed to maintain peace. Yet the 18th century was full of warfare. How does one reconcile these two statements?

The answer has to do with the prevention of hegemony by any power. Thus, countries will go to war to prevent the upset of the balance, at least as they perceive it.

4. In what ways does Western Civilization in the last quarter of the 20th century resemble an "Old Regime"? Are some of the constitutional, socio-economic, and diplomatic questions which plagued the 18th century still with us?

Note the clash between conservative powers set on maintaining the world as it is and the revolutionary forces trying to bring about substantial changes.

Now let us turn to the specific subheadings of the chapter for consideration of several important details.

I. THE ECONOMIC "REVOLUTIONS"

The 18th century saw a great flourish of capitalistic development, in agriculture, in commerce, and in the early industrial revolution. Our students should consider the positive and the negative effects of these revolutions. They should consider the effects on the workers (agricultural--including slaves--and urban), on the bourgeoisie, and on the nobility, as well as on the country as a whole. Moreover, they should see the links to foreign affairs, diplomacy, and war. PRE-BUSINESS students should be challenged to consider the role of the business leader in the 18th century and the role of government in promoting and controlling business.

TO DEFINE AND DISCUSS

Lloyds of London
weights and measures
paper money vs. gold
national debt
enclosures
mercantilism

comparative advantage
social mobility
Jenkins' ear
the *asiento*
"the true balance of power resides in commerce."

II. THE ESTABLISHED POWERS

Britain and France provide an excellent opportunity to compare and contrast different forms of constitutional development, the one leading to relatively successful evolution towards liberal democracy, the other to revolution. The instructor should be careful not to oversimplify these contrasts, however, by casting them as GOOD vs. BAD. After, all, the French eventually achieved a thriving tradition of democracy as well.

TO DEFINE, DISCUSS OR LOCATE

"gentry"
"pocket" boroughs
Jacobites
Guadeloupe and Martinique
nobles of the robe
Madame de Pompadour
Spanish Habsburgs and Austrian Habsburgs
ambitions of Elizabeth Farnese.

III. THE NEWCOMERS

The rise of Prussia has long been a major topic in the history of Europe. From the perspective of the immediate post World War II period, one might have argued that it was just temporary on the European scene (like the rise and decline of Sweden). Now, with a reunified Germany with its capital once more at Berlin, it may be more immediately relevant. In any case, it is a fascinating phenomenon. This chapter does not treat Frederick the Great's domestic or intellectual achievements, but stops at 1740. However, because Frederick the Great is treated later in the chapter during the part of war and diplomacy, you may wish to give the students a bit of a preview of Frederick as a so-called Enlightened Despot (see p. 364).

Peter the Great may be familiar to some students because of movies and TV. In any case, interest in Russia is strong among American students, and they may relate Peter's forced modernization of Russia to the similar forced modernization under Lenin and Stalin.

Poland and the Ottoman Empire are portrayed as "victims." This approach presents a fine opportunity for discussion of who is "victimized" in foreign affairs and why. Neither state developed an effective structure, whether constitutional monarchy or absolutist monarchy.

TO DEFINE, DISCUSS OR LOCATE

the Great Elector
standing army
Junker class
Frederick William I
Peter the Great's brother Ivan and sister Sophia
the *streltsi*
the *boyars*
Azov
St. Petersburg
"window on the West"
industrial serfdom
"Sick man of Europe,"
librum veto
janissaries

IV. WAR AND DIPLOMACY

The 18th century wars are indeed excellent examples of the balance of power in action and therefore deserving of serious study by students in an introductory course. On the other hand, such study sometimes degenerates into a memorized list of names and dates of wars and treaties. The instructor can make some sense of all this by treating the class as a set of general staff officers planning what should be done--from the standpoint of the British, the French, the Prussians, etc.

You might ask the students why so many of the wars are called the "war of the _____ succession"? This will get them used to the idea that dynastic struggles, not national or ideological struggles, were at the heart of the conflicts. You might also remind them of the relations between American history and world history during the eighteenth century. Indeed, this was the time that major inroads were made into the North American continent by the British, French, and Spanish, so that the LOCAL HISTORY of many areas with which the students are personally familiar may be used to illustrate the great conflict of the "second hundred years' war."

TO DEFINE, DISCUSS OR LOCATE

Hanover
Scotland
Clive and Dupleix
Elizabeth of Russia
Maria Theresa
the Black Hole of Calcutta
Louisbourg
Quebec
Wolfe and Montcalm
Pitt and Pittsburgh
Frederick the Great

SUMMATION

Students may remember the activities surrounding the 200th anniversary of the US Constitution, if not the 200th anniversary of the Declaration of Independence. Relate the 18th century Old Regime, its social structure, its high politics, its arts and letters, its constitutional developments (or absence of same) and its war and diplomacy to elements of American history with which they are familiar. It was the century of the three cornered hat, and the world was extremely cosmopolitan. It was the world of Washington and Jefferson (after whom many of their schools were named) as well as the Georges and the Fredericks. It was the age of the Enlightenment.

In the 1990s the capital of Germany is once more Berlin, and the citizens of "Leningrad" have voted to have the city renamed St. Petersburg. You might get an interesting discussion going around the phrase "plus ca change, plus c'est la meme chose."

CRITICAL THINKING

The very concept of the "Old Regimes" implies that the world is on the verge of revolution. Yet in certain respects the state system and the socio-economic structure described here is already very "modern." Try to get the students thinking about the world of balance of power politics on the one hand and the world of monarchies brewing up for a revolution on the other.

17. THE ENLIGHTENMENT

The MAJOR GOAL of this chapter is to introduce the students to the ideals and ideas of the eighteenth century, often known as the age of reason, and to the political implications of this intellectual movement. Too often the history of ideas in an introductory class reverts to the memorization of names and dates, because the ideas themselves are fairly complex and insufficient class time is available to explain them adequately. Because this chapter deals with both the ideas and their political implications, that problem may be successfully overcome. Specifically, the Enlightened Despots and the American Revolutionaries each tried to carry out the ideals of the "age of reason," each with rather different effects. In lectures, discussion, and exams, this link between theory and practice should be made explicit.

The NINTH EDITION has deleted a few details on enlightenment thinkers, and added material on Mary Wollstonecraft, otherwise if follows the previous editions closely.

BASIC OBJECTIVES

1. The student should analyze what the authors mean by the terms used in the chapter headings,

Enlightenment
the *philosophes*--and philosophers
laissez-faire
enlightened despotism
Frederick the Great
Joseph II
Catherine the Great
George III

2. The student should recognize and identify (or define) the key individuals, places, and events treated in the chapter, e.g.

Maria Theresa
John Locke
Condorcet
Benjamin Franklin
Diderot and the *Encyclopédie*
Adam Smith
Voltaire
Montesquieu
Rousseau
the Declaration of Independence
David Hume
Immanual Kant

Pietism
Methodism
romanticism
Johann von Goethe

As a review, students should be reminded of the Habsburg and Hohenzollern dynasties and the concept of the balance of power in foreign affairs and checks and balances in domestic affairs.

3. Students should be helped to see the link between the ideas of the scientific revolution of the seventeenth century and the Enlightenment of the eighteenth. One way to do this would be to argue that science is basically subversive to traditional ideals, both religious and secular. In a sense the Church was right when it feared Galileo, and fundamentalists are right today when they fear Darwin. Attempts to apply a "scientific method" to matters traditionally reserved for faith is surely revolutionary. Similarly the traditional social order, such as the patriarchy, can be undermined by science and enlightenment.

4. The connection between the enlightened despots and the American revolutionaries is not at first evident, but students should be brought to see the similarities. Superficial similarities like the three cornered hats can be used as a first step toward the more significant matters of government and philosophy. Ben Franklin, Frederick II Hohenzollern, and Catherine the Great had much in common. So did traditionalists like Maria Theresa and George III.

5. This chapter gives students of American history an excellent opportunity to see the rising of the thirteen colonies from a new angle, that of world history. Students might be asked to argue the case from the British standpoint, or to emphasize the importance of the French intervention to the struggling colonies. By the same token the influence of the Americans on the Europeans' stirrings for liberty should be noted. Under Enlightenment pressure, perhaps, no throne was safe.

QUESTIONS FOR DISCUSSION AND ESSAYS

1. What did it mean to be "enlightened," or to be an advocate of the "age of reason?" What was potentially revolutionary about this philosophy?

Note the attack, either implicit or explicit, upon authority and upon traditional ideas, both religious and secular. Ben Franklin, revered as one of our "founding fathers," was a Deist, a scientist, and a revolutionary. The concept of "laissez-faire" clearly undermines the authority of traditional elites. Students who consider themselves patriotic American conservatives may be amazed at how radical our traditions are.

2. Compare and contrast the ideals and practices of Frederick the Great, renowned as an Enlightened Despot, and Maria Theresa of Austria, very much a traditionalist.

Note that it may be necessary to dip back into the previous chapter to see the diplomatic and military struggles between the two, but it is essential do so to see some of the implications of "enlightenment" in practice. Students should be reminded that Frederick saw himself as the "first servant" of the state (a modern and secular view), while Maria saw herself as the "mother" of her country (a traditionalist view). Note also that religiously Frederick was a skeptic, while Maria was a loyal Catholic.

3. The Enlightenment, in theory and in practice, had substantial limitations; discuss them, with reference both to the importance of sensibility over pure reason and to the disinclination of monarchs and their civil servants to overturn politically entrenched traditions.

Note how naive and superficial some of the optimism of the enlightenment was: society is not simply a branch of physics. Frederick or Catherine could participate happily in the intellectual life of the age, but they dared not truly reform their political structures. Nor could even the American revolutionaries; contrast "all men are created equal" with the perpetuation of slavery.

4. The contrasts set forth in chapter 15 are seen again here, with the genius vs. everyman and the progress vs. pessimism juxtapositions. Discuss the crosscurrents of the age in both intellectual life and political developments.

Note both the rationality of the philosophes and the rise of religion in the form of pietism and Methodism and of emotionalism in the *Sturm und Drang* [storm and stress]. Note the strict absolutism of the Prussians and the demands for liberty of the philosophes and the American revolutionaries.

5. Discuss the might-have-beens of enlightened despotism and revolutionaries. What if George III had been as gifted and enlightened a monarch as Frederick II of Prussia? Would there have been an American Revolution? What if Louis XV and Louis XVI had been capable of enlightened administration? What was the result of enlightened despotism in Spain, Portugal, and Sweden?

Note the inherent limitations of the system, based as it almost always was on a particular socioeconomic structure. Even if George's policies had been reasonable (and one could argue that they were) they ran against the ideals of self-government. Self-government in the hands of traditional aristocratic and clerical elites, however, could limit the power of the rational state and perpetuate the exploitation of the lower classes (like the Russian serfs) and protect the privileges of the elites.

BOXES

BOX p. 359 "Locke's Theory of Knowledge" [written record]. Locke's ideal of the mind of each and every person beginning as a blank slate, or *tabula rasa* is the basis of our modern theories of human equality.

BOX p. 361 "Adam Smith on Free Trade" [written record]. Students should see that Smith's statement is the classical liberal position, and a position that is close to that of American political conservatives today.

BOX p. 363. "The Beginning of 'Modern History'" [doing history]. In this new BOX the author grapples with the definition of "modern." Modernism is more than just a matter of chronology. It is question of approach. Treat this passage as a stimulus to discussion rather than as a definitive statement.

BOX p. 372 "The Stamp Act Congress . . . " [written record]. Here European and American history come into direct conjunction--or conflict. Will they all recall the battle cry, "no taxation without representation"?

Now let us turn to the specific subheadings of the chapter for consideration of several important details.

I. THE PHILOSOPHES AND THEIR PROGRAM OF REFORM, 1690-1776

We are all still children of the Enlightenment. The very fact that we are teaching in colleges and universities indicates our implicit dedication to its ideals. Still, we have some of the critical distance from it to see it as a failed, though noble experiment. Or is it a never-ending experiment, neither failed nor successful, with each group of students who seek to push away the clouds of ignorance and make the world a brighter place?

Of all the great minds of the Enlightenment, the key place probably belongs to Voltaire. His statement on the Deist God, quoted in the eighth edition, but deleted in the NINTH, his emphasis on toleration, and his place as the some-time confidant of Frederick the Great, keep him at the center of the chapter. Spend some time discussing him and his ideas to provide a reference point for the other thinkers and practitioners of the age. But Voltaire need not be shown just as a hero, because he had his limits as well. What do students think of his arguments for enlightened despotism over democracy? Students of French may well come into their own again here, and should be encouraged to show that their study of language has some utility.

TO DEFINE AND DISCUSS

Locke and the *tabula rasa*
Madame de Pompadour and the *Encyclopédie*
the Physiocrats and economics
Cesare Beccaria and torture
Rousseau and education
Montesquieu and the constitution

II. ENLIGHTENED DESPOTS

Just as Voltaire can be the keystone of part I, Frederick of Prussia can serve the purpose for this section. This clever and dedicated monarch demonstrates both the strengths and weaknesses of enlightened absolutism, as some scholars are now calling the movement. The authors do a good job of pointing out the paradoxes in Frederick's behavior--such as his combination of tolerance in religion with his anti-Jewish policies. In the case of the Austrians, a nice contrast can be drawn between Maria Theresa, the traditionalist, and her son Joseph II, the enlightened absolutist. Most students, I fear, will tend to skip over the references to Spain, Portugal, and Sweden as unimportant details, but they show the widespread nature of the movement.

TO DEFINE AND DISCUSS

Frederick of Prussia and his army
Maria Theresa of Austria as "Lady Prayerful"
Joseph and Leopold of Austria as reformers
Charles III of Spain and Gustavus II of Sweden as economic reformers

The concepts of mercantilism and *laissez-faire* should be reviewed to clarify the role of the state in the economy under enlightened despotism.

III. RUSSIA, 1725-1825

The portion of this section on Catherine the Great fits in nicely with the underlying theme of the chapter, because she is often cited as an enlightened despot. Her lack of real accomplishments, of course, is the best demonstration of the limitations of enlightened despotism often mentioned. Though technically an autocrat, she could not really control the massive country and could not risk alienating the noblemen on whose support she depended.

Note how important assassination and other forms of direct violence were in Russian politics. There was no means of direct non-violent opposition, so Catherine came to the throne through violence and her son Paul was removed by murder. Your discussion of Alexander I with your students might be postponed till we meet him again in Chapter 18.

Students probably need some help with Central and Eastern European geography, so maps should be used to emphasize the partitions of Poland and the Russian gains against Turkey.

TO DEFINE, LOCATE, AND DISCUSS

service nobility
serfs
Pugachev's rebellion
Speransky's reforms
Gregory Potemkin
the Bosporus and the Dardanelles

IV. GEORGE III AND AMERICAN INDEPENDENCE

Dealing with the American Revolution in a world or European history course is both easy and difficult. There is a tendency for everyone to assume that all the "facts" at least, are already known, and that all that needs to be treated is a new interpretation. Some kind of quiz will quickly identify if the "facts" are really that well known. You might use the "define, locate, and discuss items" below for quick pre-test. Then go on to the new realm of broader interpretation.

George III had reasons to want to tax the citizens of the Thirteen Colonies, and those should be made clear to the students. On the other hand the parallels between the colonists' calls for liberty and those of English radicals like John Wilkes in England should be pointed out. If there is time and inclination, perhaps a DEBATE between the British and American sides might be in order, or at least a parallel outline of the appropriate arguments.

TO DEFINE AND DISCUSS

John Wilkes
Pontiac
the Stamp Act
the Townshend duties
the Boston Tea Party
Lord North
the Declaration of Independence and the American Constitution
Franklin and Jefferson

V. CHALLENGES TO THE ENLIGHTENMENT

The literature, the arts, and much of the intellectual life of the late eighteenth century does not fit neatly into the ideal of the "age of reason." This is an important fact to emphasize, because it avoids the simplistic view of the history of ideas which introductory students crave. Remind the students that in the eighteenth century, as in our own day, conflicting tendencies coexist. Thus the Deism of the philosophes and the fundamentalism of the pietists and the Methodists overlapped in terms of time; indeed, in a sense, they were both reactions to the formalities of established religions. So also in the arts the baroque evolved into the rococo and then was challenged by neoclassicism and even neogothic. Only pictures will make such words meaningful to the students.

The men and women of the Enlightenment, of course, loved a vigorous argument. You should remind the students that it was Voltaire who said that he might disagree with a statement, but he would defend to the death one's right to say it. Thus it is not surprising that the age saw a wide variety of ideas and styles.

TO DEFINE, IDENTIFY, AND DISCUSS

Kant's categorical imperative
Pennsylvania Dutch

nonconformist chapel
Swift's *Gulliver's Travels*
the novel
Hogarth's prints
Bach's fugues
Handel
Haydn
Mozart
Wollstonecraft's *Vindication of the Rights of Woman*

SUMMATION

The Enlightenment was dedicated to the idea that humankind could solve all of its problems by the use of human reason, but it gave birth to Romanticism with its emphasis on human emotion. Its ideals were expressed both by absolute monarchs and by republican revolutionaries, and both tried to carry out its mandates. Our students accept without question some of the ideals of the Enlightenment, especially when they are associated with American patriotism, but are shocked by others, which appear either too conservative or too radical. Here is the stuff of magnificent teaching, if one can grasp it.

CRITICAL THINKING

Critical rational thought is central to our current approach to history. Help the students see how it springs from the ideals of Enlightenment thought, but that it goes beyond it in important ways. National comparisons among Enlightenment thinkers may be useful here, and prepare students for the ages of increasing nationalism to come.

18. The French Revolution and Napoleon

The MAJOR GOAL of this chapter is to highlight the great French Revolution of 1789 and its aftermath, not only for its immediate importance for the history of one major country, France, but for its importance to the whole history of the modern world. You may wish to review the final section of the chapter, THE LEGACY OF THE REVOLUTION, to fix in your own mind the world-historical significance of this brief period of time.

On another level, this chapter treats that basic conflict in much of history (and life), the freedom of the individual verses the rights of the multitude. Does a Napoleon assure the rights of the people as a whole, or does he tyrannize over the individual?

The NINTH EDITION keeps the important new interpretive insights in the final section of the chapter on the legacy of the revolution which were added in the eighth edition. It adds significant new material on women, specifically the BOX on Olympe de Gouges. A number of details are eliminated throughout the chapter to streamline it, but the overall approach remains the same.

BASIC OBJECTIVES

1. The student should understand what the authors mean by the basic terms mentioned in the chapter sub-headings:

Clergy, Nobility, and Third Estate
the Estates General
the Gironde
the Mountain
the reign of terror
the Thermidorean Reaction
the Directory
Consulate and Empire
the Continental System

2. The students should be able to recognize and identify the key individuals, events, and places in the chapter:

Louis XVI and Marie Antoinette
the First, Second, and Third Estates
sans-culottes
bourgeoisie
suffrage
assignats
the Jacobins
Robespierre

Napoleon Bonaparte
the Concordat
Nelson and the battle of Trafalgar
the retreat from Moscow
Wellington and the battle of Waterloo
nationalism

3. The French Revolutionaries sought to achieve *liberté*, *egalité*, and *fraternité*. The students should be led to unpack those ideals and to see that in certain respects they are ultimately incompatible with one another. Thus the fact that the revolution degenerated into the Terror under Robespierre and an imperial dictatorship under Napoleon was not just due to particular ambitions and personal failings, but was in part inherent in the nature of the revolution.

4. Craine Brinton, one of the original authors of the textbook, was a great authority on the French Revolution. Even though there have been changes over the many editions of the textbook, much of Brinton's original concept has been retained. You might wish to consult his classic of comparative history, *The Anatomy of Revolution*, first published in 1938, for background.

5. The French Revolution provides especially fruitful opportunities for discussions of comparative history, particularly in classes where students can be assumed to have studied the Roman Republic and Empire. The French were self-consciously aware of the parallels, and the rhetoric of the period, as well as the art and architecture, makes it easy for students to see them as well. Even if your students have little background in classical civilization, the parallels with the English and the Russian revolutions can be usefully made.

6. There is a constant tendency to see this chapter as almost exclusively French history, but it is not. You should strive to get the students to think globally, by looking at the importance of the Americas and the impact of revolutionary ideals on the entire European world.

7. The role of slavery in the French empire, its abolition in the radical phase of the revolution, and the dramatic role of Toussaint L'Overture in Haiti, emphasizes the importance of the French Revolution of people of African descent.

QUESTIONS FOR DISCUSSION

1. What caused the French Revolution? Was it economic conditions? Was it the ideals of the Enlightenment? Did the two interact?

Note that although there were immediate economic problems, both government bankruptcy and poverty, the ideals of the Enlightenment caused leaders to denounce the injustices of the system and call for change, rather than just accept the situation as inevitable or God-given.

2. What was democratic about the French Revolution? And what was tyrannical or dictatorial?

Note the increasingly radical demands for equality on the one side, and the attempts to protect property on the other. A discussion of Edmund Burke's concerns about liberty, and Tocqueville's association of fanaticism in politics with religious fervor would help provide an informed answer.

3. Discuss the rise and fall of Napoleon Bonaparte.

Note that the Corsican is an excellent example of "careers open to talent" which often comes with revolutionary equality of opportunity. But he eventually failed because of his own megalomania and because of the reassertion of the balance of power.

4. What was the effect of the French Revolution on black people in France and the French colonies?

Here is an opportunity to deal with the racial issues which are of major importance to many American students. Francois Touissaint L'Overture of Haiti was a black revolutionary who took French ideals and used them to end slavery and establish an independent black republic in the Caribbean. Note that the Jacobins, radicals who established the Terror at home, applied the ideal of equality to people of all races.

BOXES

BOX p. 384 "Women's Rights in the French Revolution" [closer look]. This newly included document (the "written word") has rightly become very frequently used in demonstrating the importance of gender in history. Note the similarity to the "Declaration of Rights of Man and Citizen." And point to the irony in item 10--"a woman has the right to mount the scaffold"--which Olympe de Gouge ultimately did.

BOX p. 389 "The Death of a King" 'written record]. A graphic document, which can be matched with the visual on the preceding page.

BOX p. 391 ""Napoleon Rallies His Troops" [written record]. The ideals of the revolution shine through the propaganda for the "soldiers of liberty" who can "humiliate proud kings." Compare the rhetoric here with the revolutionary slogan of "liberty, equality, fraternity." Note how nationalism and liberalism are used to inspire the troops.

Now let us turn to the specific subheadings of the chapter for consideration of several important details.

I. THE CAUSES OF THE REVOLUTION

Students may expect that the leaders of France during the closing years of the Old Regime were wicked, but the chapter shows clearly that Louis XVI and Marie Antoinette were not. In a purely personal sense, they had admirable characteristics, but as the responsible leaders of a country in crisis they were clearly incompetent. Students may ask why the French monarchy, which was the powerful object of emulation by so many states during the time of Louis XIV was now in so much trouble. Excessive luxury at court was only part of the answer. More important was the fact that the monarch and the high nobility has ceased to function as a genuine ruling class.

The more sophisticated students should be brought to see how members of each of the three estates contributed to the instability of the Old Regime in different ways. Try appointing three of your more eloquent students and asking each to represent the views of one of the estates. Then complicate the picture by appointing a couple of others to represent the views of a liberal cleric like Sieyes and a liberal nobleman like Mirabeau.

TO DEFINE AND DISCUSS

Ben Franklin and the American and French Revolutions
the parlements
hoberaux
gabelle
the Assembly of Notables
the Estates General and the National Assembly
the Tennis Court Oath

II. THE DISSOLUTION OF THE MONARCHY

The fall of the Bastille, and the attribution of "let them eat cake" to Queen Marie Antoinette are two of the great moments of history from which myths are made. Indeed, students might be asked to reflect upon the importance of myth in history. The French come to believe themselves great revolutionaries, and revolution is a recurring theme in French history till today.

More subtly, the students should consider why the constitutional monarchy failed to work. Was the constitution itself to blame, or was the King of the French? Do revolutions tend to swing into radicalism and "devour their own children" inevitably? Unless there is substantial class time to sort out the various party groupings which struggled for power as the revolution swung to the left, students should be led directly to the major questions of how one establishes constitutional government and the Rights of Man in a volatile situation.

TO DEFINE AND DISCUSS

National Guard
the Bastille
the Great Fear
the Declaration of Rights of Man and Citizen
the Declaration of the Rights of Women
the Civil Constitution of the Clergy and "non-juring" priests
the *Marseillaise* (you might play a recording)
the Jacobins and the commune

III. THE FIRST REPUBLIC

As the constitutional monarchy proved impossible, calls for a radicalized republic became ever more insistent. Note the importance of radical agitators like Marat, but also of counter revolutionaries, from aristocratic emigres to simple folk like Charlotte Corday. Note the call to arms to save the nation from foreign invaders and traitors at home. Thus can the bloodshed of the terror be understood. If your students are looking for violent action, here is their opportunity--even in the art of the era, with Marat's death and the beheadings at the guillotine.

Note that the democratic spirit of nationalism inspired the French troops to feats of heroism which surprised and defeated the best troops that the neighboring monarchies could throw against them. Even the guillotine itself was a kind of a symbol of equality, because previously only the high-born had the privilege of execution by beheading. Commoners were hanged or beaten to death.

The reaction of the moderates during the Directory is also an important part of the First Republic, as is the fact that a brilliant young officer becomes a popular hero with political ambition. Financial and political corruption also soils the reputation of the republic, providing the opportunity for a popular dictatorship in the guise of a classical consulship. Students may well raise the question: how is democracy possible?

TO DEFINE AND DISCUSS

Marat, Condorcet, and Robespierre
right wing vs. left wing
the Festival of the Supreme Being
new systems of weights, measures, and calendar, giving us both the familiar (meters) and the obscure (Thermidore)
Babeuf and the Conspiracy of Equals

IV. NAPOLEON AND FRANCE
&
V. NAPOLEON AND EUROPE

The chapter now shifts to a biographical theme intertwined with diplomacy and warfare. The set of TRANSPARENCY maps, and the maps in the textbook, become very important here, lest students become as lost as some of Napoleon's troops on their way home from Moscow. You may not wish to fight through all the battles and treaties, with the ever changing borders, but you may still want to reflect on a couple of major geographical points.

Napoleonic France was far more successful in its conquests than Louis XIV's France had ever been. Surely the reason is the ideological fervor associated with the ideals of liberty, equality, and fraternity. Yet those same ideals were learned by France's opponents and turned against her. Goya's painting of the execution of Spanish patriots speaks eloquently to this point (p. 398), but it is also implied in Napoleon's own words to his troops in the BOX. The little general and grand emperor finally overreached himself with the attack into Russia, though he tried to make a comeback with his escape from Elba before his final defeat at Waterloo.

TO DEFINE, LOCATE, AND DISCUSS

Corsica
British sea power and French land power
plebiscite
Code Napoleon
Malta
Belgium
end of the Holy Roman Empire
economic warfare through blockade and Continental System
Peninsular War
German nationalism
the brothers Grimm
Stein's reforms
Czar Alexander and the retreat from Moscow
Wellington and Bluecher at Waterloo

V. THE LEGACY OF THE REVOLUTION: *SUMMATION*

This brief reflection, with the new material on women and the common people added for the eighth edition, puts the complexities and sometimes bewildering details of the chapter into perspective. The Old Regime was unable to reform itself, and the Enlightenment had set forth ideals of rationalism, natural rights, and justice. These are still summed up for us in the slogan of liberty, equality, and fraternity. In a sense Napoleon, in his heroic fashion, realized all that was both great and dangerous in those words. Patriotism became virtually a new religion, fanatically forcing itself on the non-believers. The worst of Edmund Burke's predictions seemed to come true. But though Napoleon was defeated and the revolution apparently discredited, the Old Regime could not be put together again. In the nineteenth and the twentieth century demands for liberty and national self-determination would grow in spite of reactionary repression.

CRITICAL THINKING

None of the previous chapters concentrate so directly on a single generation's history. The Great French Revolution is not only one of the turning points of world history, it is a model against which all subsequent revolutions are measured. Thus your students will find it worth their time to ask and attempt to answer penetrating questions about it.

19. ROMANTICISM, REVOLUTION, AND REACTION

The first half of the nineteenth century demonstrates an almost Hegelian dialectic between the reactionary governments of Metternich's Europe and the revolutionary challenges of the 1820's, 1830's, and 1848. The MAJOR GOAL of this chapter is to clarify this sometimes confusing period for the students. The notion of Romanticism, which itself sometimes defies rational definition, helps to square this particular circle. Students who themselves sometimes feel that they are romantic revolutionaries, repressed by a conservative society, may well take to this period with unexpected enthusiasm.

The NINTH EDITION eliminates a number of details from previous editions, adds some material on the revolutionary independence movement in Latin America. It follows the same approach as previous editions, but in a somewhat streamlined fashion.

BASIC OBJECTIVES

1. Students should be able to analyze and explain the major terms in the subject headings of the chapter.

the romantic style
Congress of Vienna
Serbia and Greece
Decembrists (Russia)

2. The student should recognize and be able to identify, define, or locate the following major items treated in the chapter.

reaction (or reactionary) and counterrevolution
sensibility and emotion
nationalism and liberalism
Herder's <u>Volksgeist</u>
Hegel's dialectic
Metternich and Talleyrand
Shelley and Wordsworth
Louis XVIII of France
Belgium
July Monarchy
Mazzini and Cavour
<u>Zollverein</u>
Big Germany and Little Germany
Monroe Doctrine

3. Although the first half of the nineteenth century in most of Europe was a time of reactionary governments, the chapter emphasizes

revolutionary activity. Students should be brought to an understanding of the mutual interaction of revolution and reaction.

4. When looking at European history, there is a tendency to associate nationalism and conservatism, placing them both on the "right wing." Students should understand that nationalism was generally a liberal movement in the nineteeth century, and nationalists thought of themselves liberating their nations from imperial domination. By the same token, a conservative reactionary like Metternich hated and feared nationalism. Students will understand this conjunction if you recall for them the link of liberalism and nationalism in the French Revolution on the one hand and the link of nationalism and "liberation" in Asia and in Eastern Europe more recently.

5. In most of the chapters of this book cultural history is relegated to the end of the chapter, but here it goes at the beginning. There is good reason for that, since the key concept is a cultural one-- Romanticism. Perhaps you should start any discussion or lecture on the period with the cultural life as well. Play a bit of a Beethoven symphony, or relate the romantic tale of the tortured lover on the way to the gallows which lies behind Berlioz's "Symphonie Fantastique" (noting the cartoon on p. 407).

BOXES

BOX p. 406 "Shelley on the Decay of Kings" [written record]. The drama of romanticism is doubly clear in this famous passage. Romantics were fascinated with the past, often long hidden beneath the sands of time, literally or figuratively. Moreover, there is a revolutionary message here, warning kings of their impermanence.

BOX p. 413 "The Monroe Doctrine" [written record]. This well known topic in American diplomatic history is put into a world context here. The new edition cuts a sentence referring to the power of the British fleet, which helped to make Monroe's statement realistic. If Britain had opposed Monroe and the U.S. the proud "doctrine" might have come to nought.

BOX p. 422. "Literature and Historical Analysis" [doing history]. This chapter reinforces the importance of literary sources for understanding history; this is a new BOX from Charles Dickens's *Hard Times*. Part of this material was used in the industrial revolution chapter in the previous edition. Remind the student's of Dickens's Scrooge, so they have some context, however Americanized, for understanding the passage. Notice that the author refers to Dickens as a "satirist and social critic."

QUESTIONS FOR DISCUSSION

1. In what way was the period one of reaction and in what way was it one of the struggle for liberty?

Note that the one is really the reverse side of the other. Metternich and his allies feared the ideals of liberty, equality, and fraternity and set up their governments to repress such ideas, even in their moderate form. Reactionary governments were sometimes so absurd and repressive (like Polignac's in France) that they inspired revolutionary responses.

2. Why did Metternich and his supporters fear nationalism, and why did the nationalists consider themselves liberals?

Note the chart showing the breakdown of the Habsburg monarchy by nationalities (p. 421), and be sure to explain that the nationality groups were intermixed in such a way that there could be no rational way to draw boundaries between them. The conflict between the Serbs and the Croats should be firmly in people's minds. Similarly, the German-speaking people were split up among Austria, Prussia, and numerous smaller principalities. Italians were divided in the same way.

3. Recount the major goals of the revolutionaries of 1848 and consider how and why they failed to achieve their goals.

Note that the nationalists, the liberals, and the working classes each opposed the old order for differing reasons. They could unite to attack the monarchies, but once the monarchies had fallen (or had temporarily retreated), their goals diverged and they fell to fighting among themselves. In many cases the old order retained enough strength to reassert itself when the opportunity arose.

4. Was Romanticism a liberal or a conservative movement?

Note that it was basically a question of style, which could be adapted for various goals. The emphasis was on emotion rather than reason. To the conservative that meant a reverence for tradition and the rejection of the rationalism of the Enlightenment. To the liberal (and the revolutionary) it meant a desire for freedom, the attempt to throw off all restraints, and the willingness to endure any sacrifice to achieve revolutionary goals. Delacroix's painting, "Liberty at the Barricades," (p. 417) conveys the revolutionary Romantic, while the restoration of Notre Dame de Paris, or the neo-Gothic Houses of Parliament in London symbolize more conservative Romanticism.

The recent popularity of the musical version of Hugo's *Les Miserables* may help many of your students relate to this period.

Now let us turn to the specific subheadings of the chapter for consideration of several important details.

I. The Romantic Protest

Slides and recorded music, or even better, a field trip to a neo-Gothic local building or to a live musical performance, constitute possible ways to introduce this chapter. Students who are well versed in literature will also have a good idea of what Romanticism means. There are short definitions of the word, of course, and the major concept--defining it in terms of its opposite, rationalism--is not difficult. But the depth of feeling of the Romantic movement is not easy to convey.

Try using words like love and hate, and ask the students to define them rationally.

Although the concept of Romanticism is treated most clearly in this particular chapter, be sure that students realize that cultural movements are not easily limited by boundaries of time or space. Romanticism goes back into the Enlightenment, with Rousseau, and continues on into the twentieth century.

TO DEFINE AND DISCUSS

Schiller and Goethe
Coleridge's "Kubla Khan"
Pushkin
Victor Hugo
Goya
Turner
Hegelian idealism
the idea of the *frisson*, cold thrill

II. THE RECONSTITUTION OF A EUROPEAN ORDER

Edmund Burke's critique of revolution, and Metternich's fears about political order, both need to be discussed, because most students will get little from them without such a help. Students might be reminded that Americans have been seen as the conservatives in a revolutionary world; contrariwise, American ideas of liberty made some of the Communist states which fell around 1989 seem "conservative." Those who remember who Henry Kissinger is (and was), may be interested to know that he wrote one of his first books on Metternich.

Some Americans might dismiss the men and women who supported the Metternich system as hopeless reactionaries. But they should be reminded how much the world had suffered under the wars brought on by the democratic idealism of the French Revolution. Moreover, they should note that the balance of power set up by Metternich endured for nearly a century. It was not a century of total peace, of course, for there were many small wars. But none of those wars were as lengthy or destructive as the Napoleonic Wars or World War I.

TO DEFINE AND DISCUSS

Bourbon restoration
Holy Alliance
Carbonari
Guizot and Thiers
the Carlsbad decrees
Ultramontanes
Serbs and Croats

III. THE REVOLUTIONS OF 1830
&
IV. THE REVOLUTIONS OF 1848

At last the revolutionary tide overflowed the reactionary dikes built by the Metternich system. 1830 was partially successful in the West, where traditions of revolutionary democracy could bring crowds into the streets. 1848 seemed to do the same for the central European states, particularly in the German and Italian states. Yet in every case--and students may wish to consider if this is not inevitable--the revolutionaries fell short of their goals.

Though it would to be a great shame to ignore the smaller states, you may wish to emphasize the developments of the French and the Germans in these two revolutions. The French, in spite of their revolutionary heritage (or because of it?) proved unable to establish a constitutional democracy at this time. A new Napoleon emerged instead. The Germans expressed high ideals, but proved unable either to unify their people or to create a lasting liberal constitution. One historian suggested that 1848 was the "turning point which failed to turn."

In part, of course, it is a myth that all the central European '48ers eventually came to America to establish our democracy. Yet there are some interesting individuals whose careers followed that path. More significant for European development is the reaction against political Romanticism which followed the failures of 1830 and 1848; both revolutionaries and conservatives moved in the direction of "realism" in politics. High ideals were not enough; one had to have power.

Marching bare-breasted over the barricades may be heroic, but one is likely to get shot.

TO DEFINE AND DISCUSS

Charles X of France
Louis Philippe (the" citizen king")
Flemings and Walloons in Belgium
Polish nationalism
Burschenschaften
July Monarchy and June Days in France
Risorgimento
Mazzini
the Frankfurt Assembly
"Big Germany" vs. "Little Germany"
Magyars and Czechs
Louis Kossuth
Piedmont

SUMMATION

With the new emphasis on social history in the profession, much of the political activity described in this chapter may seem divorced from reality. But the disruptions of the industrial revolution, which was sweeping much of Europe during the years covered here, helps make the whole period more understandable. Industrialism will be treated in detail in the next chapter. At some point you will want to introduce your students to the ideas of Karl Marx. Not, heaven forbid, to make converts, but to let them know about how so many of the educated and powerful men and women in the world have viewed history. Metternich's world was also Marx's world, and one might argue that your students cannot understand the one without the other.

CRITICAL THINKING

You and your students might like to grapple with the perennial question of "when modern began?" The early 19th century, with its ideals of liberal nationalism, democracy, and romantic idealism, introduces more of those elements into the cultural and political mix we think of as modern. Then, it may be useful to turn to the question of why some revolutions succeed and why some fail. The period is full of examples, and they will be fleshed out further in the next chapter on the Industrial Society. Note that failure or success of revolutionaries has something to do with the revolutionaries themselves, but also a good deal to do with the health or weakness of the governments they are trying to overthrow.

20. THE INDUSTRIAL SOCIETY

The MAJOR GOAL of this chapter is to analyze with the students the development and impact of the industrial revolution in western society. Thus this chapter stands outside the general chronology of the nearby chapters, reaching back to the late eighteenth century for the beginnings of the Industrial Revolution in England, and moving to the end of the nineteenth century with its various "isms." Social and economic history, and its accompanying history of ideas, therefore, is the subject of this chapter.

The NINTH EDITION cuts a number of details and quotations from the previous editions to make the chapter more efficient, an appropriate goal for a chapter on industrial society. Among the items deleted are BOXES with selections of John Stuart Mill's *On Liberty* and Charles Darwin's *Origin of Species*.

BASIC OBJECTIVES

1. All students should understand and be able to describe what the authors mean by these terms in the chapter subheadings.

stages of industrial (or economic) growth
limited liability
population explosion
liberalism
classical economics
utilitarianism
humanitarian liberalism
utopian socialism
Marx and Engels
Christian socialism
anarchism
Darwinism and Social Darwinism
racism
idealism and realism

2. The student should recognize and be able to identify the key individuals and related items in the chapter.

Eli Whitney
Bessemer converter
Stephenson's Rocket
the Rothschild brothers
abolition of the Corn Laws
Saint-Simon
Benjamin Disraeli
Malthus and Ricardo
Bentham and Mill

Charles Dickens
Charles Fourier and Robert Owen
Kropotkin and Proudhon
Popes Pius IX and Leo XIII
Charles Darwin
Cecil Rhodes

3. When the industrial revolution is discussed in a history textbook, the great technological strides are often emphasized but the immediate effects of these improvements are sometimes ignored. Like all revolutions this industrial revolution had its victims, and even those who ultimately befitted from it had substantial prices to pay.

4. As in the intellectual history presented in the former chapters, the ideas here can be seen as a range, or even a clash of ideas. Remind the students that Marx and Dickens were concerned with some of the same social problems, but their approaches were very different. Marx came out of the Enlightenment tradition and sought rational explanations and scientific formulas to solve the problems. Dickens appealed to the emotions, as a person closer to Romanticism. The more sophisticated students will see how "idealism" and "realism" will fit into all this.

5. This chapter will demand a reassessment of the class structure for the students. Marx introduces some new terminology--proletariat and a new definition for bourgeois. The Industrial Revolution itself, along with the French Revolution, ended the domination of the old aristocracy which has been with us since the Middle Ages.

QUESTIONS FOR DISCUSSION

1. What was revolutionary about the Industrial Revolution?

Note the substitution of mechanical power for human and animal muscles, the importance of iron and steam, and above all the vast increase in productivity. Then consider the implications of these changes for the lives of the people, the working classes and the upper classes as well.

2. Create arguments both in favor of, and against, the following proposition: "the Industrial Revolution improved the lives of the workers wherever it went."

Note how the authors are carefully balanced in pointing out the positive and negative effects of the Industrial Revolution. Note the statistical discussion of birth rates and death rates, as well as the more personalized stories and the pictures in the textbook.

3. Compare and contrast the responses to industrialism by liberals, socialists, and conservatives.

Note both the grim "realism" of the economic theorists and the humanitarian liberalism of Dickens and Mill. Note the utopian and the "scientific" socialists. Note the responses of the Catholic Church, in many ways the most conservative of institutions, but still expressing charitable concern.

4. Describe and critique the theory of history set forth by Marx and Engels.

Note the origins of Marx's thought in the Enlightenment search for laws of nature, but also in an ethical reaction to the evils of slums, child labor, and the business cycle. After having learned the "lessons" of the French Revolution, Marx and Engels expected the workingmen of the world to unite to throw off their "chains." But they did not do so (or at least not as Marx predicted). Some references back to the Revolutions of 1848 from the previous chapter will be helpful here.

BOXES

BOX p. 433 "The Experience of Immigration" [closer look]. The authors use a brief document expressing dismay at the poor health of immigrants to North America as a springboard to a critique of anti-immigration sentiment. You might wish to ask your students if they see any anti-imigrant manifestations in the news of the day. You might also ask them where they might be now if immigration to North America had ceased in the year 1800.

BOX p. 436 "A Day at the Mills" [written record]. This transcript from a governmental hearing in 19th century England helps students to understand the impact of industrialization on family life. Have them note the picture of a mill on p. 429 and the picture of working class homes on p. 439.

BOX p.445 "Pope Leo XIII Attacks Socialism" [written record]. Note how this traditional institution, the church, criticizes both reolutionary socialists and exploitive capitalists.

BOX p. 451 "The Song of the Shirt" [written record]. What other examples from British (or European) literature can your students recall which help the comfortable to sympathize with the laboring poor?

Now let us turn to the specific subheadings of the chapter for consideration of several important details.

I. STAGES OF INDUSTRIAL GROWTH

British industrial growth is shown here as the model of general growth into industrialism. But it is not simply unlimited growth, but eventual decline as well. Students would do well to ponder the significance of that fact, because many of them seem to be be uncritically convinced that the United States has always been, and will always be, the most powerful industrial nation on the globe.

The international links of the economy, and the links between agriculture and industry, are nicely set forth in this part of the chapter. With luck you will have students from both the US and abroad in your class, or from urban and agrarian roots, so that they can relate these discussions to their personal experiences.

TO DEFINE, IDENTIFY, AND DISCUSS

global economy
stages of growth
inflation
depression
Samuel Morse
Justus Liebig
Irish potato famine

II. ECONOMIC AND SOCIAL CHANGE
&
III. THE RESPONSES OF LIBERALISM

Students commonly talk about the standard of living, but this chapter should give it more meaning for them. Find out which of them has experience in factory work, or even the assembly line of a fast food operation. Get their views on the the Iron Law of Wages, and the operation of the other economic "laws." Many of them will have had some exposure to basic economics in previous classes. Some may be pre-business students who have (or think they have) a sophisticated understanding of the "dismal science."

Some may wish to turn the discussion into an evaluation of the US political scene of today, and that might be a mistake. But it is important for them to be able to identify "classical" liberalism with today's laissez-faire conservatives. It is also important that they see how utilitarian ideas can be applied to improve conditions for real people.

You might wish to discuss the importance of industrialization for women and for family life. Remember that John Stuart Mill was as advocate of women's rights, as well as for liberalism in general.

TO DEFINE, IDENTIFY, AND DISCUSS

urbanization
capitalism
population growth
mortality rates
middle classes
wage labor
pauperism
Bentham
nature vs. environment argument
Mill's *On Liberty*
social engineering

IV. SOCIALIST RESPONSES: TOWARDS MARXISM
&
V. APOSTLES OF VIOLENCE AND NONVIOLENCE

When Marx and Engels wrote the *Communist Manifesto* early in 1848, they were responding to a particular set of socio-economic and political circumstances, as well as to broader movements in the history of thought. Thus the utopians and the classical economists are an important part of the story. In some cases your students will be so prejudiced with an anti-communist ethos that they will have trouble understanding what Marx and Engels were even disturbed about. In other cases you may still have some students who see Marxism as the ideology which, in theory, can solve all problems of the world. In either case you have a vital and challenging task to show that Marx and Engels really thought that they had the "scientific" solution to the real social problems which surrounded them, and that their theories made some sense in that context. Let us leave the question as to whether they still make sense today to another time.

The attempt to sort out the definitions of socialism and communism on p. 440 is very useful, particularly now after the fall of the USSR.

TO DEFINE AND DISCUSS

New Lanark and New Harmony
Fourier's phalanx
Louis Blanc
the Hegelian dialectic
Das Kapital
August Blanqui
Bakunin
anarcho-sydicalism
the *Syllabus of Errors*
Rerum Novarum

VI. A NEW AGE OF SCIENCE
&
VII. LITERATURE AND THE ARTS IN INDUSTRIAL SOCIETIES

Scientific, pseudo-scientific, philosophical, and literary ideas tend to blend together in this era. If Darwin's own writings are not "Victorian literature" (and one might argue they are), then the themes of the Social Darwinists certainly were. Nietzsche and his concept of the "superman" fits well into the themes of idealism, realism, and elitism; Hitler's racism comes later, of course, but the way has been laid. Painting and the performing arts, on the other hand, tend to fit more naturally into the discussion of Romanticism and its various competitors as set forth in the previous chapter.

TO DEFINE AND DISCUSS

atomic theory
natural selection

survival of the fittest
Herbert Spencer
eugenics
Rhodes and imperial racism
Compte and positivism
antirational will
Zola
Turgenev
George Bernard Shaw
Walt Whitman
photography and impressionism
Wagner's "music dramas"
Mark Twain

SUMMATION

If you cannot get a good discussion going with a chapter encompassing the ideas of both Marx and Darwin, then you must have a tough class indeed. If all else fails, divide them up arbitrarily into Marxists and Darwinists (for an hour or so) and stage a debate. See which workers will lose their chains and which of the fittest will survive.

The collapse of Communist regimes in Eastern Europe over the past few years raises the question of the theoretical value of Marxism. Does the collapse prove Marx was wrong, so we can consign his ideas to the scrap heap of history (like Ptolomey's astronomy)? Or does the collapse merely show that the Communist Parties were simply reading Marx wrongly? The political events of the late 1980s and early 1990s may require a significant revision of historical interpretations in general. Or, perhaps the Communist parties, in reformed garb, will make a comeback. Unregulated capitalism has not been a complete success in Eastern Europe.

CRITICAL THINKING

The rise, and eventual decline, of a major industrial power (Britain) should be an important story for the critical consideration of North Americans looking at their own place in the world. The attempts of thinkers to develop theories and practices to deal with the pitfalls of unregulated capitalism should be an important story of the critical consideration of people around the world. Was all socialism ultimately Utopian? Or was it based on an ultimately realistic Iron Law, a law of nature rooted in creative conflict? Students, who are citizens and will be leaders, should apply their intelligence to these matters.

21. THE MODERNIZATION OF NATIONS

The MAJOR GOAL of this chapter is to show the students a comparison of six major states of the world as they entered the twentieth century. This is comparative history, and the format COMPARE AND CONTRAST may be used to good advantage. Be careful, however, that the students do not see these all as "nations." Indeed, two of the six were not nation-states, but multi-national empires; three of the six suffered defeats and lost territory during the twentieth century; five of the six underwent revolutions. Modernization can be painful.

The NINTH EDITION has been shortened by the deletion of some details of fact and of some of the analysis. The maps showing the unification of Italy and Germany have been eliminated. New material on women's history has been added, particularly concerning German and the United States.

BASIC OBJECTIVES

1. Students should have a clear grasp of the words used in the chapter subheadings. Some of these are geographical terms, so the use of maps--TRANSPARENCIES, wall maps, or the MAPS in the book itself--is essential.

France's Second Empire and Third Republic
nation-state
Imperial Germany
Dual Monarchy
intelligentsia
Duma
Civil War and Reconstruction (U.S.A.)

2. Students should be able to identify, locate, or define the key items from the chapter.

welfare state
Realpolitik
manifest destiny
Captain Dreyfus
Garibaldi
Otto von Bismarck
Reichstag
Spanish American War
William II
Panama Canal
anti-Semitism
Zionism
populism
Francis Joseph
Crimean War

Franco-Prussian War
Russo-Japanese War

3. Students tend to take our democracy for granted, so much so that they often neglect to vote. They tend to see democracy as the normal and proper form of government for a modern nation-state. In this chapter they can see the varieties of constitutional developments toward democracy. Germany is often seen as the homeland of authoritarianism, but in terms of the breadth of franchise and in terms of social legislation it was sometimes ahead of France and Britain, not to speak of the United States with its treatment of non-whites. Austria-Hungary made several attempts to establish representative parliamentary institutions. Even Russia, after 1905, made a gesture in that direction.

4. The growth of the great powers in the late nineteenth century was partly a matter of power politics and partly a matter of industrialism. Students should be able to relate this chapter with the previous one to be able to see how the politics and the socioeconomic questions are intertwined.

5. Modernization theories often stress that there are both positive and negative impacts of modernization. Our students tend to think uncritically that MODERN=GOOD. Use the materials in this chapter to give them a more balanced view.

QUESTIONS FOR DISCUSSION

1. Compare and contrast the nineteenth-century developments toward a liberal and democratic nation-state in France, on the one hand, and Italy and Germany on the other.

Note that 1848 "failed" in each case, but that the French had already solved its nationality problem and more or less set its boundaries, while Italy and Germany had to face both the national unification problem and the constitutional liberal-democratic problem at the same time.

2. Discuss the nationality problem in the Habsburg Empire, including treatment of Italians and Germans well as the Magyars, Jews, and Croats and Serbs.

Note the nationalities map as well as the written text.

3. Compare and contrast the constitutional developments in the three great imperial dynasties of the Hohenzollerns (Germany), Habsburgs (Austria-Hungary), and Romanovs (Russia).

Note that we are speaking more and more of nation-states as we approach the twentieth century, but that dynasties and their interests are still with us. Dynasties may be anachronistic, but they are nevertheless powerful up to World War I.

4. Current events may well give you a chance to show the relevance of aspects of this chapter which may, at first, seem like trivial details. For example, note the continuing struggles in the former Yugoslavia. I expect that ethnic tensions in Central Europe will continue over the life of this edition, a regrettable situation, but one which history can help us understand.

BOXES

BOX p. 464 "Eating Well in the Nineteenth Century" [written record]. The menu for the "three emperors" is perhaps not so remarkable in itself. If one visited a fine restaurant in Paris today, similar fare is to be found. What is astounding is to compare it with the food eaten daily by the average Parisian of that day.

BOX p. 472 "The Growth of Bureaucracy" [closer looks]. This section from a well known German sociologist, with an introductory analysis by the authors, introduces one aspect of the modern state. How many of your students have had frustrating experiences with a bureaucracy of some kind? And how many of them will find careers in some private or public bureaucracy themselves?

BOX p. 492 "The Influence of Sea Power" [written record]. Captain Mahan's warnings are doubly useful in this chapter. Not only does he call attention to the importance of modern steel and steam navies for the twentieth century in general, he shows how the Untied States has no choice but to be part of the power structure of the modern world.

Now let us turn to the specific subheadings of the chapter for consideration of several important details.

I. FRANCE: A SECOND EMPIRE, A THIRD REPUBLIC

The French habit of numbering its governments can help the students get a handle on the unfolding of French political and constitutional history. Refer them to the FIRST and SECOND Republics, and the FIRST Empire, as well as noting that we are now in the era of the FIFTH Republic.

By now the students should have the idea that the French look upon themselves, with some reason, as a nation with a great military tradition. That tradition, and the shock of the defeat by the Germans in the Franco-Prussian War, helps us to understand the French in the twentieth century. But they also, by the late nineteenth century, have developed a great revolutionary tradition. This chapter treats them both.

TO DEFINE, LOCATE, AND DISCUSS

Louis Napoleon Bonaparte (Napoleon III)
Paris and city planning
birth control and population
Maximilian of Mexico

Alsace and Lorraine
Zola and the Dreyfus case

II. ITALY AND UNION, 1849-1870

Cavour's brilliant combination of the ideals of the liberal nation-state with shrewd diplomacy and political manipulation contrasts sharply with the idealism of the earlier Italian nationalists, like Mazzini. We must not forget that this is the land of Machiavelli. The book introduces the German term *Realpolitik* here, and with good reason.

Remind the students of the ideals of the *Risorgimento*, but also of the problem based in the fact that the papacy was an Italian political institution at that time. Also, it is vital to remind them that the reality of unification did not match up with the optimistic projections of the utopia it would bring. That is an important point, because it applies as well to many of the non-European countries who gain their "freedom" in the twentieth century.

TO DEFINE, LOCATE, AND DISCUSS

Garibaldi
Victor Emmanuel II
Camillo Cavour
Piedmont-Sardinia
Lombardy
Naples
Sicily
Venetia
Ethiopia (Abyssinia)
the "Roman question"

III. GERMANY, THE NATION-STATE

Bismarck's manipulation of the German Confederation into the German Empire through three wars and domestic discord is a magnificent tale, from which people can draw all the wrong lessons. Surely many Germans did so in the twentieth century, much to their ultimate distress. The "blood and iron Chancellor" was not merely a spike-helmeted dictator, but a politician and a diplomat who knew how to manipulate the forces of his time to his personal advantage and to the advantage of the Hohenzollern monarchy. This edition keeps the caption to his picture calling him "the pragmatic German chancellor" and deletes the "blood and iron" quotation.

But the new German Empire could not remain forever under the clever leadership of Bismarck, and it permanently changed the balance of power in the European world. When William II sought to secure his country's "place in the sun" he challenged the status quo in a way which ultimately brought on World War I, though that was not his goal. That war ended the brief glory of the German Empire.

When the seventh edition was published, one might have argued that German "unity" in its Bismarckian sense was only a brief historical phase. Now with the NINTH EDITION Germany is reunited (minus territory lost in World War II) and Bismarck's Berlin, without a wall, is once more the capital.

TO DEFINE, LOCATE, AND DISCUSS

Denmark and Schleswig-Holstein
Bavaria
the German civil war
the Ems telegram
the Franco-Prussian War
Kulturkampf (recall Canossa from the Middle Ages)
the Social Democratic Party
Berlin-Baghdad railway
Frieda Duensing
Admiral Tirpitz
Max Weber

IV. THE HABSBURG EMPIRE: DIVIDING HUMANITY INTO NATIONS

To approach this question we must begin with a map, and the one provided on page 478 and on the transparency of NATIONALITIES IN CENTRAL AND EASTERN EUROPE is excellent. Show the students where the Habsburg Empire (or Danubian Empire, or Dual Monarchy) lies. Then explain that even this map is highly oversimplified and that there are many minorities within minorities all over that "tossed salad" of a state. The map shows now distinction between Croats, Serbs, and Bosnians, and the Jews, everywhere a minority, do not show on the map at all.

Though the nationality problem seemed hopeless, and eventually touched off World War I, the Habsburg monarchy provided the context for a rich and varied social and cultural life, giving us Sigmund Freud and a host of modernist artists, musicians, and literary figures.

TO DEFINE, LOCATE, AND DISCUSS

Bohemia
Czechs and Slovaks
Magyars and Hungary
Croats, Serbs, Bosnians and Slovenes
Poles, Ruthenians, and Romanians
Dalmatia, Herzegovina, and Montenegro
Karl Lueger
Lajos Kossuth

V. RUSSIA, 1825-1914

Now we dip back, chronologically, to pick up the story of the Russian Empire, sweeping over a century to the eve of the Russian Revolution. Appropriately the chapter is generally divided by the reigns of the Czars, beginning with Nicholas I and ending with his namesake, Nicholas II. Note that when looking to the other countries, no longer under the domination of a royal house, the chapters are not divided primarily with reference to royalty. Yet the seeds of the Russian Revolution are here too, with discussions of the Marxist groups and of Lenin himself.

War and diplomacy plays part of the story as well, with the Crimean War and the Russo-Japanese War. Students might wish to consider whether it might have been possible for the Russian autocracy to reform itself into a constitutional monarchy, along the models of the British or Scandinavians. But, you must remind them (unless some of them are quick enough to remind you) that the British had their revolution in the seventeenth century, so that the development of British democracy was anything but a smooth evolution.

TO DEFINE AND DISCUSS

serfdom
zemstvos
Slavophiles and Westerners
nihilist
populist
Tolstoy
pogroms
Bolshevik and Menshevik
Revolution of 1905 (rather like 1848 in Central Europe)
Stolypin's reforms

VI. THE UNITED STATES: MODERNIZATION AT TOP SPEED

Depending on your students, and how much United States history they have had, you may or may not wish to spend much time on this part of the chapter. What is important for them is to see the development of their own country in comparative perspective with the developments of other major countries. Thus the Civil War is seen as "an abortive nationalist revolution." It also makes sense to compare it with the wars of national unity in Germany and Italy. Russia, still an autocratic state, freed its serfs two years before the United States freed its slaves.

From the standpoint of foreign affairs, we should also keep United States history in perspective. We have already noted French participation in the war for American Independence. In the nineteenth century the War of 1812 was really part of the Napoleonic Wars, and the United States got involved in the New Imperialism with the Spanish American War and our "open door" policy in the Far East.

TO DEFINE AND DISCUSS

Monroe Doctrine
Mahan and sea power
Lincoln
Theodore Roosevelt
Woodrow Wilson

SUMMATION

Modernization, it can be argued from the evidence in this chapter, is a two edged sword. Progress certainly was a major force in the late nineteenth century; a glance back at the previous chapter, which included British developments in the same period makes that even more clear. But progress toward what?

CRITICAL THINKING

Students might develop their analytic skills by making a grid comparing the impact of modernization on each of the major states and their peoples discussed in this chapter. The questions posed on page 494 make it relatively easy to do this. National unification, industrial development, minority questions, struggles to democratize both politics and society, all these are comparable. Comparability, of course, does not mean equivalence, as your students will soon see.

22. MODERN EMPIRES AND IMPERIALISM

The MAJOR GOALS of this chapter are to familiarize the students with two intertwined subjects, nineteenth-century British history and the development of the New Imperialism. Britain is seen as the model, both for internal modernization and democratization, and for overseas empire. Imperialism is seen in both its positive and negative aspects, an approach which might seem odd to some of our students, for some of whom "imperialist" may be a kind of political cuss-word. But, perhaps enough time has passed since the liberation of the colonies after World War II for even the new nations of the world to recognize that there were some positive aspects to their years under colonial domination.

The NINTH EDITION abbreviates some of the details, especially in colonial history, and it adds information and interpreting on feminism and women's history in Britain.

BASIC OBJECTIVES

1. The student should recognize and understand the major terms used by the authors in the chapter sub-headings.

two-party system
Utilitarians
the Irish problem
New Imperialism
Dominion status

2. The student should be able to identify, locate, or define the major items mentioned in the chapter.

postindustrial economy / postmodern history
protective tariffs/free trade
representative government
Corn Laws, and repeal of the Corn Laws
Queen Victoria
Whigs and Tories / Liberals and Conservatives
the Great Reform Bill, 1832
Disraeli and Gladstone
depression of 1873-1896
welfare state
"Fabian" socialism
nature-nurture debate
Eastern Question
Durham Report
Boers and the Boer War
Suez Canal
Mohandas Gandhi

assimilation
Manifest Destiny
Perry in Japan
Spanish-American War
Panama Canal
samurai
Russo-Japanese War

3. The history of western civilization becomes world history in this chapter, even while maintaining its Eurocentric approach. Students will need to have maps always before them, lest the "far away places with strange sounding names" will bewilder them. Nevertheless, a major objective of your course should be to make them as comfortable as possible in our global village, and this chapter gives you the opportunity to develop that process.

4. There is an inherent contradiction in the fact that Britain is at once democratizing internally, but also extending its colonial rule throughout the world. The same might be said of France and the United States. To some imperialists this contradiction was resolved by reference to the "civilizing mission" of empire. Hopefully your class will be multi-ethnic itself, so these materials may have to be handled with some diplomacy.

5. Though you might be a bit unhappy that all the non-British empires are relegated to the catch-all category of "other," you nevertheless have the opportunity to use the COMPARE AND CONTRAST analysis to deal with various empires. Most important here, given recent world events, are the opportunities to treat Japan, South Africa, and the United States informal empire in the Caribbean.

QUESTIONS FOR DISCUSSION

1. Describe the unfolding of British constitutional monarchy during the nineteenth century, from a parliamentary oligarchy to a democracy.

Note that the constitutional monarchy, with ultimate parliamentary supremacy, was already in place because of the revolutions of the seventeenth century; the only major question was the matter of who would get to control parliament. This was a matter of no small significance, of course, but a much easier problem than those faced by the continental countries (Germany, France, Italy) who were also struggling along the same road toward democracy during the same period. Chartists passed petitions while revolution and counterrevolution wrestled on the continent.

2. Discuss the interaction of democratization and imperialism, using the British experience as your major example.

Note that some imperialists saw the empire as a way to keep the working classes at home in support of the government, while some anti-imperialists denounced the government in the name of the people for expensive adventurism. At the same time, ideals of nationalism and democracy are picked up by the non-Europeans from the Europeans themselves and turned against the "mother country."

3. Compare and contrast the empires of the major European states with those of the two major non-European states which developed empires during this period, the United States and Japan.

Note the longer traditions of the British and French empires (though not the German and Italian). In several respects the Japanese took their cues directly from the Europeans, while the Americans showed considerable ambivalence, because of their own heritage of anti-colonialism. Thus American imperialism was developed as informal empire and, even more than by the Europeans, was justified in terms of "liberating" the peoples under its "protection." Note the Open Door policy and the Spanish-American War in this context.

4. Two categories of colonies often cited for purposes of analysis are "settler" colonies and "non-settler" colonies. Describe the two, with examples, and consider the implications for the post-colonial period in each case.

Note the more permanent nature of the settler colonies, which may indeed develop into self-governing dominions in the image of the "mother country" like Canada and Australia, if the native peoples of the area are few and weak. On the other hand, if the native peoples are numerous and strong, as in South Africa, the potential for bloody conflict is great (as in Algeria). Non-settler colonies, like India, have an easier time gaining independence, because the colonials just "go home."

5. Describe Lenin's theory that imperialism is the highest stage of capitalism, and apply it critically to the development of the New Imperialism.

Note the importance of economics, and particularly investment, to the New Imperialism, as well as the potential for conflict between the great imperial powers. On the other hand, note that things did not exactly turn out as Lenin predicted, any more than they did as Marx and Engels predicted just before the revolutions of 1848.

BOXES

BOX p. 504 "Beatrice Webb on 'Why I became a Socialist'" [written record]. Note that humanitarian concerns and moderate goals were characteristic of her approach, rather than the Iron Law of Wages or a call for revolution. Have our students considered public education as "socialist"?

BOX p. 508 "Kipling's View of Imperialism" [written record]. There are magnificently mixed messages in this poem, the condescending racist references to "heathen folly," and the stark realism of "the savage wars of peace." Try asking the students to unpack this poem in terms of race, class, and gender.

BOX p. 510 "Technology and Empire" [closer look]. This BOX is lengthened from that in the previous edition, and it provides a wonderful opportunity to compare with Kipling's "white man's burden" statement.

Now let us turn to the specific subheadings of the chapter for consideration of several important details.

I. BRITAIN, THE FIRST MODERN NATION, 1815-1914

The impact of the industrial revolution, studied earlier, now takes political form in looking in detail at British politics. The struggle over the Great Reform Bill of 1832 was, in a sense, the British form of the Revolution of 1848; or, to put it another way, the reform rendered the revolution unnecessary.

Still, one should not idealize the situation in Britain. Readers of Dickens' novels, or the reports of the various parliamentary commissions, know that there was widespread suffering among the working classes. Anyone who follows the domestic career of Wellington, or the situation in Ireland, knows full well that harsh repression was not excluded from the British approach to problems.

Nevertheless, the Victorian politeness of the alternating governments of the Conservative Disraeli and the Liberal Gladstone seems much more in character, and more in line with our generally positive views of modernization and progress. The good sense of the Utilitarians, the functional adequacy of the two-party system, and movement toward some kind of social service state, are the hallmarks of modernization, British style.

TO DEFINE AND DISCUSS

Oxford and Cambridge Universities
expanding suffrage
poor laws and poor houses
Kier Hardie
Joseph Chamberlain
David Lloyd George
Shaw and the Webbs
Ulster
the Catholic Emancipation Act of 1829
Irish Home Rule

II. THE GREAT MODERN EMPIRES AND THE QUESTION OF IMPERIALISM

Students may ask what was new in the New Imperialism, and one would do well to consider the implications of their question, that what was new 100 years ago might not seem so different from the "old" imperialism today. Yet in terms of ideology, capability, and extent, the imperial movement of the late nineteenth century was notable indeed. Simple notions of mercantilism were replaced by much more elaborate and subtle economic interests, whether "free trade" or "imperial preference." The industrial revolution, and the accompanying medical and weapons technology, made it possible for Europeans, Americans, and Japanese, to dominate vast areas of the globe, some 84 per cent at least for two or three generations. Leninist critics seized on the exploitive side of this outburst of imperial zeal and developed the anti-imperialism which dominates much of the world today. But most important of all was nationalism, both for the imperialists and for those seeking to throw off its control.

Now is the time to turn to the MAPS in the book, or the TRANSPARENCIES supplied, to introduce your students to the globe. If your school has some dusty old World War II era wall maps, get them out, as historical documents. Point out how the names have changed since the turn of the century, with Rhodesia and its like replaced, just as the rulers of the old empires have been replaced.

III. THE BRITISH EMPIRE
&
IV. OTHER EMPIRES

When one looks at the British Empire, as it unfolds in this chapter beginning with Canada, the sharp distinction between the old and new imperialisms seems inappropriate. To be sure, the loss of the Thirteen Colonies cast something of a pall over the enthusiasm for empire, but the lesson was learned in London, and the white settler colonies were permitted, little by little, to establish a new relationship to the mother country. That came to be known as Dominion status. The newest author of this textbook has a strong background in this field of history, so the book gains added authority on the topic.

The story of the Boers, the Boer war, and the current situation in South Africa come together to provide useful discussion materials. Many Europeans developed a pronounced sympathy for the Boers during the Boer War, so roughly treated were they by the British at the turn of the century. After World War II, however, it was the Boers (usually called Afrikaners) who were the staunchist proponents of apartheid and white supremacy. Some of your students may not realize that the Boers were white, so their origins in the old Dutch empire should be explained.

The rise of Japan, and its complex relationship with the United States, deserves special attention. The material for that consideration is here, but it may have to be highlighted to busy students who find it tucked in at the end of a long chapter, and treated more briefly than Canada. The Japanese, once they opened to the West, did so in a well organized fashion, taking technology, military organization and weaponry, and constitutional forms from the different Western countries.

TO DEFINE, LOCATE, AND DISCUSS

Belgian Congo
Malaya
Bantu and Zulu
Gold Coast
Cape Colony
Islam in Africa

Chinese Empire
the mahdi and Gordon at Khartoum
Fashoda
Falkland Islands
the Sepoy Rebellion in India
French North Africa
French Indochina
Battle of Wounded Knee
Hawaii
"remember the Maine"
concentration camps
Cuba as an American protectorate
Korea and Japan
China and Taiwan (Formosa).

SUMMATION

Two aspects of the New Imperialism which link it closely to the increasingly popular governments of the late nineteenth century were Christian Missions and naval strategy. Missionaries were motivated by high ideals, no doubt, but many of them had narrow ideas of what "the good" was, and sought to impose them on peoples with complex and admirable cultures of their own. In some cases non-Europeans were able to blend the best of both worlds, but in other cases the only results of the missionizing were negative for all concerned. Naval strategy was a very important aspect of the empire building of the age, whether it meant cutting canals to link the seas or securing island bases far in the midst of vast oceans. In each case, Christianity and navalism were popular with the folks back home. In an age of democratization such popularity was politically valuable.

CRITICAL THINKING

The idea of a balance sheet on the good and bad effects of imperialism fits in nicely with the concept of the British as a "nation of shopkeepers." The economics of imperialism does lend itself to such rational analysis, and that would be a useful exercise for your students. Your pre-business students, especially those who hope to be employed by multi-national corporations, should try their hands at it. But students should also apply their critical faculties to the problems of imperialism which go well beyond budgets. Ideals of nationalism and freedom are as important to non-Europeans as to Europeans.

23. GREAT WAR, GREAT REVOLUTION

The MAJOR GOAL of this chapter is to familiarize the students with those upheavals which most still World War I and the Russian Revolution. The authors are quite right to retain the older names, because the adjective GREAT emphasizes the vast magnitude and crucial importance of these two events, rather than implying some moral worth. Even from the 1990s, nevertheless, people will argue that these cataclysms deserve the titles GREAT.

The NINTH EDITION has cut a number of political, military, and diplomatic details to streamline the chapter. The approach and general interpretation, however, remains the same.

BASIC OBJECTIVES

1. The students should understand and be able to demonstrate their understanding of the major concepts used in the subheadings.

Triple Alliance
Triple Entente
Lenin
the November [October] Revolution
War Communism

2. The student should be able to identify, locate, or define the key individuals, places, and concepts of the chapter.

Bismarck's Three Emperors' League
ententes
the Balkans
Serbian nationalism
the "blank check"
the Schlieffen plan
trench warfare
submarine warfare
the Dardanelles
the Ottoman Empire
British sea power
Ludendorff and Hindenburg
war propaganda
Wilson's Fourteen Points
The Treaty of Versailles
self-determination of peoples
the League of Nations
Poland
Nicholas II, Alexandra, and Rasputin
the March [February] Revolution

Trotsky and Stalin
Bolshevik Reds and anti-Bolshevik Whites

3. Historians have spilled a great deal of ink looking for the long term and immediate causes of the Great War. Yet all of the research and analysis should not lead the students to the conclusion that the war was inevitable. At least it was not inevitable in 1914, and exactly who would fight on whose side was not determined with certainty till the guns began to fire. In a brief survey the Triple Alliance and the Triple Entente look clear and firm, but they were not. The German hoped they could keep the British out of the war until the war actually began, while the Italians did not go to war at all in 1914 and ended up fighting with the Entente powers rather than with their erstwhile allies.

4. Some students may still look naively on the Soviet Union as our major potential enemy, and therefore see the Russian Revolution as an unmitigated disaster. By now, however, they have the historical background to see the events of 1917 in context. Not only do they see why Russia was ripe for revolution (even without Lenin and Leninism), but they know something about the nature of revolutions from studying the British and French experiences. You might also ask if they have seen any examples of uncritical praise of the revolution from pro-Soviet propaganda. The collapse of Communist domination and the USSR will also provide the opportunity for discussion. Taking Craine Brinton's analogy, did Gorbachev initiate a kind of Directory (as in the French Revolution)? Will a "Napoleon" follow?

5. The mass society of the early twentieth century at war was terrible to behold. Transportation and communication technologies made possible far higher casualties than ever before. War propaganda among democratized, or partially democratized, peoples called them to ever higher levels of sacrifice. Nationalistic hates and fears led them to greater exertions. Students should come to see what was "great" in the "great war" and the "great revolution," and see why the optimism of the eighteenth century and much of the nineteenth could be seen as misplaced. Mass produced goods and services can create mass destruction and death.

QUESTIONS FOR DISCUSSION

1. Article 231 of the Treaty of Versailles clearly laid the blame for the war on German aggression. In retrospect, was that an historically accurate explanation of the cause of the war?

Note both the long term and the immediate causes for the war. The rise of Germany disrupted the balance of power and made possible, or even probable, that the other major powers would fight to limit her strength. The immediate incident initiating the war took place in the Balkans, and did not involve Germany directly. But the Schlieffen plan, designed to break the "encirclement" of Germany, widened the crisis into a general war.

2. What impact did the Great War have on the home front in the various countries? Can it be said that war, win or lose, creates revolutions?

The social history of Europe was drastically altered by the Great War. Note the winners saw increasing democratization, and a greater role for women; the losers, of course, collapsed in the several revolutions.

3. Compare and contrast Europe of 1914 with the Europe which was created by the Treaty of Versailles.

Note that this is a map question [use the TRANSPARENCIES], but only partly. Political changes and economic changes were vast as well. The Russian Revolution can be seen here in context.

4. The Russian Revolution occurred in two phases, one in the spring and one in the fall. Consider why this was so, and the interrelationship between these phases and the war which was raging in Europe at the time.

Note the spontaneous nature of the Febraury/March revolution and the carefully planned struggle which brought the Bolsheviks to power in October/November. Lenin was not even in the country in the spring; the Germans let him return, for their own reasons.

5. We call the Great War by the name "World War I." To what extent was it really a "world" war, and what is the implication of the numeral?

Note that there was warfare around the globe, and eventually all the powers were involved--including Japan and the United States. But most of the fighting was in Europe. Some authorities see World Wars I and II in Europe as two phases of the same conflict, a new "Thirty Years' War."

BOXES

BOX p. 533 "The 'Blank Check'" [written record]. This is an excellent example of the kind of "behind the scenes" document that historians like to find to discover "history as it really was." Are there such confidential documents illuminating the causes for other more recent wars? Does the document "prove" that Germany alone was responsible for the Great War?

BOX p. 540 "War in the Trenches" [written record]. Develop the idea of the impact of the war on the survivors as well as on the dead. In a sense they were all casualties. Some references to the "war poets" have been cut in this edition, so you may wish to supplement the text at this point if you have the time and inclination.

BOX p. 548 "Simple Errors: The West and Russian History" [doing history]. You may ask your students to bring in materials from the daily press on discoveries about the former USSR as the archives open and historians and journalists find more confidential information about the Russian revolutionaries and the governments which operated in their name.

BOX p. 550 "Lenin's Address at the Finland Station" [written record] Students may wish to reflect on the "greatness" of Lenin, and his role in the revolution. How does he compare with Cromwell, or with Robespierre?

I. CAUSES OF THE WAR

The role of nationalism and public opinion is correctly stressed, and quite rightly the diplomatic background is traced back to Bismarck. Use of the TRANSPARENCY MAPS, or simple sketch maps on the blackboard or overhead projector will help the students see the various relationships.

For the final crisis a chronological list of events may help the students sort out the chain of cause and effect. For those who like to have staged discussions a mock trial of the German kaiser for having started the war might be instructive.

TO DEFINE, LOCATE, AND DISCUSS

revanche
Morocco crises
the Balkan Wars
Dreadnought battleships
Winston Churchill
Belgian neutrality
the *Lusitania*
American creditors

II. THE COURSE OF THE WAR
&
III. THE HOME FRONT

You might wish to draw up a balancing chart to compare the resources of the two sides:

CENTRAL POWERS	ALLIES
150 million people	275 million people plus colonial empires

which you could enhance further with economic statistics from the chart in Chapter 22. This will help to show why the Germans felt they had to take risks, like the Schlieffen plan and unrestricted submarine warfare, in order to win.

Historians vary widely on their beliefs about how important military history is in a survey course. Probably these views have something to do with how they feel about war in general. But whether or not you want to deal with battles and statistics, there should be no doubt in your students' minds that the war had a massive impact on modern history, not only for its military outcome, but for how it accelerated certain trends in domestic history.

TO DEFINE, LOCATE, AND DISCUSS

the Marne
machine-gun nests
tanks
poison gas
Brusilov offensive
Caporetto
Gallipoli
Mustafa Kemal
Bulgaria and Romania
Armenians
T. E. Lawrence
Jewish national home
Unterseeboot
total war

IV. THE PEACE SETTLEMENTS

Wilson's hope to "make the world safe for democracy" has been ridiculed by many sophisticated commentators, but it was a goal which had a good deal of meaning at the time. Indeed, it is probably fair to say that in the eyes of most Americans this phrase defines the most important goal of United States foreign policy throughout the twentieth century. The question is, of course, how could the use of American armed force achieve that goal? What would have been necessary, and did the United States and its associated countries have what was needed to accomplish the goal?

Wilson's Fourteen Points are quoted in full in the text, and they would make the basis for an interesting discussion. Students might compare them with the actual outcome at Versailles. On the other hand, students should realize why the British and particularly the French wanted a punitive peace.

TO DEFINE, LOCATE, AND DISCUSS

Treaty of Brest-Litovsk
Liebknecht and Luxemburg
Turkey and Greece
American occupation of Russian ports
the Big Four: Wilson, Lloyd George, Clemenceau, Orlando
reparations and John Maynard Keynes
Saar Basin
Polish corridor
new successor states to Austria-Hungary: Czechoslovakia, Yugoslavia
new successor states to the Russian Empire: Estonia, Latvia, Lithuania, Finland, Poland
new successor states to the Ottoman Empire: British and French mandates, Iraq
Japanese gains in the Far East
"irreconcilables" in the United States Senate opposed to the Treaty of Versailles

V. THE RUSSIAN REVOLUTION OF 1917

Just as there were other possible outcomes for the diplomatic crises prior to the Great War, there were other possible outcomes to the constitutional crisis brought on in the Russian Empire by that war. Until recently, to hear the spokesmen of the former USSR tell it, there could have been no victor but the Communist Party. You have the opportunity to explain about the other options which were available to the Russians at that time and why Lenin and his party emerged victorious.

One of the great paradoxes of the Russian Revolution was that Lenin, by all accounts one of the greatest Russian leaders of any age, pushed through a revolution which, according to Marxist-Leninist theories, should have occurred inevitably. In your discussions you might address this paradox and consider the roles of GREAT leaders on one hand and impersonal forces on the other. Would Marx have recognized the revolution carried out in his name?

TO DEFINE AND DISCUSS

old Russian calendar
Social Revolutionaries (SR)
Social Democrats (SD)
Constitutional Democrats (Kadets)
Kerensky
provisional government
Kornilov coup
the civil war
kulaks
"all power to the Soviets" vs. "all power to the constituent assembly"
Pilsudski and the Poles
murder of the czar and his family

SUMMATION

The reference to the singing of the *Marseillaise* when Lenin arrived at the railway station in Petrograd brings to mind the links between the French and the Russian Revolutions. Look again at Brinton's classic of comparative history, *The Anatomy of Revolution* to help you ponder this relationship. The Great War helped to bring about the Great October Socialist Revolution. Indeed, that was perhaps its most lasting result. The governments created by the war and the treaties which ended it are now gone, including the USSR. Is the world safer for democracy?

CRITICAL THINKING

The coming of World War I, the war itself, and the Russian Revolution, are now laid bare for historical analysis. Students should use their critical skills to determine, as closely as possible, just what happened and why it happened the way it did. What are the limits of historical knowledge? What lessons, if any, can be learned from the study of these events?

24. BETWEEN THE WARS: A TWENTY-YEAR CRISIS

The MAJOR GOAL of this chapter is to introduce the students to the concepts of authoritarianism and totalitarianism as set forth in the dictatorships of Mussolini, Stalin, Hitler, and their lesser imitators.

The NINTH EDITION abbreviates the chapter editorially, and deletes some of the pictures and the BOX quoting Hitler. Otherwise it is virtually unchanged.

BASIC OBJECTIVES

1. Students should be able to demonstrate an understanding of the concepts mentioned in the chapter's subheadings.

Fascism
corporate state
world depression
racism
Iberia
authoritarianism
successor states

2. Students should be able to recognize and correctly identify the major items of the chapter.

Benito Mussolini
fasci
Mare Nostrum
the "vital lie"
"stab in the back" legend
Ebert and the Social Democrats
Weimar constitution
German inflation (1923)
Adolf Hitler and *Mein Kampf*
anti-Semitism
the SA and the SS
Lebensraum
Francisco Franco
Austrian *Anschluss*
Lenin's NEP
Stalin vs. Trotsky
kulaks and collective farms
five year plans
charismatic leadership

3. While concentrating on the major states of central and eastern Europe, this chapter also deals with several smaller states. You might take this opportunity to discuss with your class the importance of the smaller states, both as examples of certain types of development and as countries important for their own sake.

4. The word "totalitarian" has become rather controversial among scholars, particularly as it has been applied to the Communist states, because critics charge that its use unfairly tars the left with the ugly brush of the radical right. Thus you will note that the term "authoritarian" is used when describing the Stalinist regime. Perhaps now that Gorbachev and other leaders of the new Russia have given the green light to the revelation of Stalinist crimes, the word "totalitarian" will reappear in the literature. In any case, when students read this chapter they will see that post-Great War Europe was not really "safe for democracy."

5. There is a good deal of controversy among historians and political scientists as to whether "fascism," (lower case) was a generic type of ideology which appeared in various forms (such as Nazism), or whether each of these forms was so unique that it makes little sense to pretend there was a generic form at all. For purposes of teaching, I have found that it is useful to set forth the generic ideologies (fascism for the radical right and communism for the radical left) and then deal with specific cases.

QUESTIONS FOR DISCUSSION

1. Compare and contrast the dictatorships of Mussolini and Hitler on the one hand with that of Stalin on the other.

Note the BOX by Klaus Epstein, emphasizing that while both regimes were repressive, the far right was reacting against the ideals of the Enlightenment while the far left--in theory at least--was seeking to carry out its concept of equality.

2. We fought the Great War to "make the world safe for democracy," and we won. Why, then, was democracy so strongly challenged?

Note the war had severely weakened those groups which are needed to make democracy work, both in the victor Italy, and in the loser, Germany. Democracy had not really yet had a chance in the USSR or in most of the smaller states.

3. A number of smaller European states [and states around the world] adopted and adapted the ideologies and practices of the fascist and communist leaders to their own countries. Why might they find these undemocratic approaches useful in their countries?

Note that democracy requires an educated populace, not merely in a formal sense, but in the sense of democratic ideals. Even then it is sometimes slow, awkward, and sometimes corrupt. Totalitarian and authoritarian regimes appear to be able to act quickly to deal with crises and to maintain a semblance of law and order.

4. No dictator can take and maintain power by force alone in the modern world; there must be at least some attractive aspects to a regime for it to remain long in power. What was attractive in the regimes of Mussolini, Hitler, and Stalin?

Note that each of these men had charismatic abilities and acquired a reputation for solving problems by being tough. Each played on the prejudices and idealism of their people. Note the importance of thought control and propaganda.

BOXES

BOX p. 559 "Comparing Fascism and Communism" [closer look]. The BOX combines two from the previous edition, the quotation from Mussolini and the analysis of historian Klaus Epstein.

BOX p. 561 "Ten Commandments for Fascists" [written record]. This document sounds so ridiculous today, that you must help your students to understand why anyone could have taken it seriously in the 1930s. Perhaps reference to the heroic picture to the Nazi student on p. 570 will help.

BOX p. 582 "The Dangers of Backwardness" [written record]. Notice the nationalistic appeal by Stalin, who presumable believed in Communist internationalism. Does this document give a hint as to why there is some nostalgia for the Stalinist days in post-Soviet Russia?

I. THE FIRST TRIUMPH OF FASCISM: ITALY

Many students, remembering World War II, may automatically assume that Italy had been allied to Germany during World War I as well. They must be reminded, therefore, that Orlando was one of the victorious Big Four at Versailles. It is all the more surprising, therefore, that Italy was so disrupted by the war that its constitutional monarchy collapsed and Mussolini took over.

To help explain this, point out the economic burden of the war, the heightened sense of nationalism, the difficulties of making democracy work in a sharply divided society, and the charisma of Mussolini. For those of the students with a more sophisticated understanding of ideology, you may discuss the relationships among nationalism, capitalism, socialism, and syndicalism in Mussolini's background and in his ideal of the corporate state. For those who are fans of professional football (or, even better, professional hockey) you can relate the successes of Fascist Blackshirts to the attractiveness of violence.

TO DEFINE AND DISCUSS

Gabriele d'Annunizo
the *fasci di combattimento*
militarism

the march on Rome
the Roman question
Fascist expansionism

II. THE WEIMAR REPUBLIC: GERMANY, 1918-1933
&
III. GERMANY UNDER HITLER, 1933-1939

The rise and fall of Adolf Hitler seems to retain a fascination for American students. And well it should, both because it has much to do with the shape of the European world after World War II and because the story itself holds a lesson Americans would do well to understand. Divided Europe, Soviet expansion westward and United States presence in Western Europe, are the direct effects of Hitler's war. More important, perhaps, the Hitler story reminds us of how much evil is possible even from a country which has reached the very heights of Western civilization.

Students should understand that neither the failure of Weimar democracy nor the rise of Hitler were inevitable. Yet they happened, perhaps less because of the strength of the villains than because of the weakness and apathy of the "good folks." Once in power Hitler had to be physically defeated to be removed, either from the inside or internationally. The racist ideology of the Nazis led logically to the genocide of Auschwitz. To say that it could happen again is not merely rhetoric.

TO DEFINE AND DISCUSS

the "war-guilt" clause of the Treaty of Versailles
the Free Corps
putsch
President Hindenburg
Dawes Plan and Young Plan
Der Führer
the *Volk* and the Nuremberg laws
Gestapo
Christian opposition to Nazism

IV. AUTHORITARIANISM IN IBERIA
&
V. SUCCESSOR STATES TO THE HABSBURG EMPIRE
&
VI. OTHER AUTHORITARIAN REGIMES

There is considerable debate among historians as to whether the word fascist ought to be applied to the right wing undemocratic regimes of these smaller countries. In some cases the local leaders used the word themselves, when Mussolini and Hitler were at their zenith, but abandoned it once these practitioners began to decline. In other cases the word is used as a Marxist category and a political cuss-word, as when the demonstrators called the police "fascist pigs" during the 60s.

However these debates come out, your students should have a firm idea that the European states which emerged after World War I had a great deal of difficulty establishing democracies. Indeed, the heritage of right-wing dictatorship is still important throughout the world. Some map work will be useful here as well, comparing the boundaries of 1920 with the nationalities map and the maps of 1914 and 1945.

TO DISCUSS, LOCATE, AND DEFINE

Anarchism and Marxism
Popular Front
Falange
Salazar
Dollfuss and Schuschnigg in Austria
Horthy and Hungarian revisionism
Croats and Serbs in Yugoslavia
Pilsudski in Poland
Romania and Bulgaria
Metaxas in Greece

VII. THE SOVIET UNION

Students of revolutions have long wondered what would have happened in the USSR had Lenin not died at a relatively early age, or had Stalin not defeated Trotsky in the ensuing struggle for power. Such speculations are not mere fantasies, because the more recent history of the USSR under some leaders who attempted more openness show us that Stalinist repression--"totalitarianism" if you wish--may not be inherent in Soviet Communism. On the other hand, some argue that ever since the days of the first czars only strong central leadership, and a disregard for personal liberty, could modernize Russia. You might remind the students of Peter the Great.

However one approaches the problem of civil liberties under the Communist Party of the USSR, it is vital to remind the students that Russia was a largely underdeveloped society suffering from the depredations of World War I and the internal civil war when the Communists took over. And, though this is getting ahead of the story, large scale destruction of human and material resources was the case in World War II as well. Thus any modernization at all was rather remarkable. It is even more remarkable if one assumes the inefficiency of a centrally planned socialistic economy.

TO DEFINE AND DISCUSS

socialism vs. communism
Bukharin
Stalin and "socialism in one country"
Politburo
collectivization of the farms
five-year plans
Stalin's purges

"agitprop"
Russian nationalism

SUMMATION

The placing of the discussion of the authoritarian states after The Great War before the discussion of the democratic states seems to imply a priority for the opponents of democracy. That was probably not the intent of the authors; after all it was the democratic states who won the war, and the 1920s was largely dominated by them. Perhaps you will want to assign Chapters 24 and 25 together so that students will see the parallel developments rather than dealing with the fascists and Communists first. Nevertheless, if your students come away with the view that Wilsonian optimism about the victory of democracy in 1918 was somewhat misplaced, then they will have a more realistic view of how World War II came about.

CRITICAL THINKING

As we approach today, the chapters deal in greater detail with the history of the world in which we live. Moreover, the issues of the 1920s and 1930s are still, to some degree, the issues which occupy us today. As a critical-thinking exercise, have students bring up current affairs problems in the daily press and see if there are direct parallels from the material in this chapter.

25. THE DEMOCRACIES AND THE NON-WESTERN WORLD

There are two MAJOR GOALS of this chapter: to describe the Western democracies between World Wars I and II, and to survey the non-western world during the same period. The emphasis in the portion on the democracies is how they tried to meet the challenges of the economic problems of the interwar period. When turning to the non-west we see two thrusts: anti-colonialism in most of the world, and expanding colonialism of its own in the case of Japan.

For the NINTH EDITION changes have been limited to the elimination of certain minor details, and the addition of some material on Korea. The BOX on the British Union of Fascism has be deleted.

BASIC OBJECTIVES

1. Students should show an understanding of the following terms as they are used in the chapter subheadings.

Conservative and Labour Parties in Britain
Commonwealth
the Popular Front
United States isolationism
the New Deal

2. The students should be able to define, identify, or locate the following major items from the chapter.

nationalization
Ramsay MacDonald and Stanley Baldwin
Winston Churchill
unemployment
coalition governments
Irish Republic and Ulster
Raymond Poincaré and Léon Blum
American "normalcy"
women's suffrage
Kellogg-Briand Pact
Great Depression
Social Security Act
Japanese militarism
Sun Yat-sen and the Koumintang
Chiang Kai-shek
Hindus and Muslims in India
"Mahatma" Gandhi
Arab nationalism
Zionism
Mustafa Kemal Atatürk

3. If the world as a whole was not safe for democracy after 1918, the students should realize that democracy did make substantial strides in the major Western states. Women received the vote, labor unions were recognized as a legitimate part of economic life, and various aspects of a social service state were accepted in the major countries. But all these things did not happen without substantial political struggles, and even some violence in the streets. Fascist-style groups appeared in France and Britain. The pressures of the Great Depression cut further into the laissez-faire state which these countries inherited from the nineteenth century, particularly in the United States.

4. On paper the British and French empires emerged newly strengthened from the Great War. League of Nations mandates in the Middle East gave colonial civil and military administrators new opportunities to spread the "glories" of Western civilization. But the seeds of national self-determination had also been spread by the winds of war, and nationalistic movements were gaining strength throughout the empires on which the sun never set.

5. In the case of Japan several things were happening simultaneously. Emulating the Western powers, Japan was seeking to increase its colonial and neo-colonial position in the Far East. The nationalism which undercut Western power reinforced Japanese expansionism. As the fascist and authoritarian states appeared to gain the leadership in Europe, Japan's internal development moved in that direction. The relationship between Japan and China, those two great non-western countries, is especially significant in the interwar period.

QUESTIONS FOR DISCUSSION

1. Describe the growth of democracy in the major countries of the West, noting how each built on the traditions of its own nation.

British parliamentarism worked reasonably well, while in France the Third Republic was weakened by parliamentary instability. In the United States normalcy was fine as long as the economy held. But it could not cope with the Great Depression, and people turned to Roosevelt for a New Deal.

2. What did economic conditions have to do with the policies in the major countries of the West, both domestic and foreign?

Immediately after the end of the war a period of readjustment put all the economies under great strain. Even winners had trouble readjusting. Attempts to make the Germans pay for the war, which seemed at first attractive to the victors, did not yield positive results. Relative prosperity during the mid-twenties brought relative domestic tranquility, but when the Great Depression hit something new was needed--national coalition, popular front, or New Deal.

3. What was the result of The Great War on the sense of colonial domination which had been felt by the major powers prior to 1914? And how were the colonies reacting?

Note the establishment of the British Commonwealth of Nations, in an attempt to remake the Empire in a new form. But note also that the rest of the world no longer was willing to submit to colonial rule, as signified by the followers of Gandhi in India or of the Irish Republicans closer to home. Though the chapter does not provide the detail, much the same could be said of the French and American empires.

4. During this period some countries maintained and enhanced democracy, while others lost it to authoritarian leaders. Why did democracy thrive some places and not others?

This question will involve the previous chapter as well. Note that the easy answer is that democracy was older in the Western countries and did not have sufficient roots in those to the east. There is some truth to this, but it may be overly simplistic and lead to a feeling of artificial superiority on the part of Americans. If the United States had been faced with the losses and humiliation which the Germans felt, could it have fallen to a Hitler?

BOXES

BOX p. 593 "Why Women Shouldn't Be Allowed to Vote" [written record]. The case for women's suffrage seems so self-evident now, that is amazing how long it took countries to recognize it. Have your students note that Germany and Russia gave women the vote before the United States did so (though only by a couple of years). This BOX has been shortened from the eighth edition

BOX p. 595 "FDR's First Inaugural Address" [written record]. This vigorous speech, with its famous "fear itself" line, was given by a man who was incapable of walking without help. Could a disabled person run for an win the presidency today?

BOX p. 601 "Democracy at the Village Level" [written record]. Gandhi, British-educated and a skilled lawyer, returned to the most basic of skills to bring leadership to his country. Note how he connects democracy, independence, the economy, and traditional crafts.

BOX p. 602 ""Naming and Nationalism" [doing history]. Students might compare this BOX with the one on page 8. What names have been changed over the past few years, and what has been the political significance of those changes? St. Petersburg?

Now let us turn to the specific subheadings of the chapter for consideration of several important details.

I. GREAT BRITAIN
&
II. FRANCE

By the 1920s both Britain and France had achieved the status of political democracies, but neither had solved the economic problems of an industrial (and ultimately post-industrial) age. Major strikes spilled over into violence. Ideologically polarized electorates were difficult to unite around a viable government. We think of the British having a two party system, but in reality they had three--Conservatives, Liberals, Labourites--which divided and redivided on major issues, such as the Irish question and armaments. In France the situation was complicated by a multi-party system which brought little stability to the government. Students (and many of the professors) despair of understanding a system in which the names were often misleading. The Radical Socialists, for example, were neither radical nor socialist, but rather a moderate party of the *petite bourgeoisie*.

If there had been no external threats to these countries they might well have worked out their political and economic questions peaceably. Or, one might argue that it was only under the pressure of outside threats that the British got together on anything. The French, alas, never did, and the Third Republic fell to the Germans in 1940.

TO DEFINE AND DISCUSS

"khaki election"
protective tariffs and imperial preferences
general strike
Sinn Fein
Eamon De Valera
Statute of Westminster
Ruhr occupation
petite bourgeoisie
communist-socialist split
Action Française
"better Hitler than Blum"

III. THE UNITED STATES

Without appearing unpatriotic, you should try to give the students some feeling for how relatively minor the sacrifices of life of limb were for the United States in World War I, compared to the other major participants. Some statistics should do it: 115,000 United States dead compared to 1,385,000 Frenchmen. Thus recovery from the war was not the problem for us that it was for the Europeans. Nevertheless most Americans felt politically burned by the war. We refused to joint the League of Nations and lapsed into isolationism. [Notice the dramatic difference after World War II.]

Yet America remained the ideal for many people throughout the world. We limited immigration drastically and established tariff barriers. The world depression was dramatic in its effect in the United States, and ultimately we became involved in World War II as well.

TO DEFINE AND DISCUSS

"wets" and "drys"
Allied war debts and German reparations
"the business of America is business"

stock market crash
RFC/NRA/FDR
Good Neighbor policy

IV. THE EAST MEETS THE WEST: WESTERN HISTORY AND WORLD HISTORY

The title of this book, *A History of Civilization*, implies that the West is civilized and the non-west is not--or at least it was not at one time civilized in the same way. Yet in the twentieth century one cannot avoid world-wide history. This portion of this chapter recognizes the interlocking fates of West and East.

By concentrating on three great non-western countries one can get some clarity when moving outside the more comfortable confines of Europe and North America. And each of the three shows a somewhat different face. The Japanese are emulating the West, in both its positive and negative aspects; indeed one can argue that Japan shows all that was good and bad about the West but in double time. The Chinese, long convinced of their superiority, were slow to react against Western domination. When they did react, it was with many failures, and the revolution begun in 1911 still has born only limited positive fruit. It is instructive to note that Sun Yat-sen is celebrated as a great hero both in Beijing, by people we once called the "Reds," and in Taiwan, by the descendants of Chiang. India, with its heritage of communal discord (Muslim vs. Hindu) but also with its devotion to Gandhi the nonviolent revolutionary nationalist, eventually has become the world's largest democracy.

The Middle East, then as now, was filled with contradictions, passions, hopes, and despair. This chapter should help to give students some vital background to the struggles between Arab and Zionist and among present day countries like Iran, Iraq, Kuwait, and Saudi Arabia.

TO DEFINE, LOCATE, AND DISCUSS

Military dictatorship"have not" country
Comintern
Manchuria and Manchuko
Hindu vs. Muslim
"secret of Swaraj"
Anatolia
Reza Shah Pahlavi

SUMMATION

In retrospect, the interwar period seems like only a "twenty years' truce" which divided a new "thirty years' war." At the time there were many who predicted that a new war was on the horizon, and many who tried to do what they could to prevent it. But hindsight can be misleading; it is the curse of the historian to know in advance how the story comes out. Would more imaginative leadership in the West have preserved a world safe for democracy without a renewal of the Great War? That is worthy of discussion with your class.

CRITICAL THINKING

"World history" in some sense of those words, has always existed. Yet in our secondary schools and colleges the tendency is to concentrate on "our" history, i.e. American history and the history of Western Civilization. You might put some of your students to work on the question of whether all history should be taught as global history. What would be gained? What would be lost? Would students be better educated and better citizens?

26. THE SECOND WORLD WAR AND ITS AFTERMATH

The MAJOR GOAL of this chapter is to familiarize the students with World War II, defined very broadly to emphasize Asia as well as Europe, and to include the period of the cold war as its "aftermath." The architecture of the chapter reflects the struggles of historians to come to grips with the contemporary world. We have little perspective on it as yet, but we cannot ignore it or give it over to political scientists and soothsayers. As an exercise you might ask your students to try different modes of periodization of the twentieth century and see what they suggest. The role of the United States comes through strongly in this chapter.

The NINTH EDITION makes keeps the important changes of the eighth edition, reflecting new research and insights, on both World War II itself, and the "cold war" world, and extends them to 1989. Though the structure of the chapter remains unchanged, therefore, you would be wise to reread it in its new format before teaching from it.

BASIC OBJECTIVES

1. The students should recognize and be able to locate or define and discuss the terms in the subheadings of the chapter.

Manchuria
Ethiopia
the Marco Polo Bridge
Anschluss
Battle of Britain
Axis
the United Nations
Cold War
the Soviet-Chinese [Sino-Soviet] split
Vietnam

2. The students should be able to demonstrate an understanding of the major events and concepts of the chapter.

"Locarno spirit"
Comintern
Social Democrats as "social fascists"
appeasement
popular front
Haile Selassie
Guernica
Neville Chamberlain
Munich Conference
Hitler-Stalin Pact

blitzkrieg
atomic bomb
Charles de Gaulle
Winston Churchill
Lend-Lease Act
Pearl Harbor
Stalingrad
D-Day
Auschwitz
the Holocaust
Iron Curtain
Truman Doctrine
Korean War
Cuban crisis
Mao Zedong
Vietnam War

3. One can argue that the massive struggle of the mid-twentieth century was like the Thirty Years' War of the seventeenth century in a couple of respects.

First, it was very hard on the civilian population. There is little doubt that more civilians were killed than combatants, partly because of the use of massive bomber fleets (and finally atomic weapons), and partly because intentionally destructive actions of the Nazis to "purify" conquered populations. The authors suggest 17 million military and 18 million civilian deaths, an estimate they consider "low."

Second, the war was really several wars going on at once. I would suggest the following outline, which more or less parallels the textbook treatment:
    1. *The Second German War* in which much of World War I on the western front with a similar ultimate outcome.
    2. *The Great Patriotic War of the USSR* in which Germany fought the USSR on the eastern front, the greatest land war in history.
    3. *The War Against the Jews*, an unprecedented war of genocide by the Nazis against a conquered people, whom they considered a "racial" enemy.
    4. *The Pacific War*, a naval and air war in which the United States defeated Japan.
    5. *The War for the Asian Mainland* which began as a Japanese war of conquest against China, became a Chinese civil war after the defeat of Japan, and went through Korean and Vietnamese phases. This was the longest of the five wars, lasting from 1931 to 1975, and indeed may resume again in another phase.

4. Looking at the "Second World War" in this way helps the students to understand the outcomes of the war. The United States did in fact win wars 1 and 4 above, but not wars 2, 3, or 5. Thus the United States emerged dominating western Europe and the islands of the Pacific--the "free world"--but not the world as a whole. The Cold War, therefore, was not the result of anyone's betrayal, but of the balance of power.

QUESTIONS FOR DISCUSSION

1. Consider the long term and the immediate causes of World War II, both in Europe and in the Pacific? How do they relate to World War I?

Note that the Treaty of Versailles left an unstable situation (even if one avoids the questions of "justice") with a great many unsatisfied national groups. Nevertheless, Hitler did not stumble into war, as one could argue the Germans did in World War I, but chose it purposefully. A more traditional leader might have been happy with the fruits of appeasement gained without war. Similarly the Japanese, after seeing that the United States would not tolerate its unchecked expansion, purposefully chose war with the United States.

2. Why did the Axis powers have the initial advantage in World War II, and how were the Allied powers able to turn the tide?

Note the advantages of *blitzkrieg* on land, on the sea, and in the air. This was the war of the internal combustion engine, which gave the aggressor the advantage of great mobility. On the other hand, the major industrial powers of Britain, the USSR, and most of all the U.S.A. had the ultimate advantage because they could produce more machines and the fuel to operate them.

3. Describe the relationship between the USSR and the capitalist democratic states of the West before World War II, during the war, and immediately after. Was some sort of conflict predictable as soon as the Nazi threat was eliminated?

Note the importance both of ideology and of classic balance of power theory. The ideology created distrust and potential hostility. The grasp for hegemony by the Nazis temporarily forced the western and the Soviet Union into coalition for balance of power purposes, but the coalition disappeared as soon as the Nazi threat was gone.

4. What was the place of the United States in the mid-twentieth century, and how does it differ from the United States's place in the nineteenth and early twentieth centuries?

Note how we could observe, or at least perpetuate the myth of, isolationism up to the mid-1930s, but since then we have had to take up our role as a major power. Our emergence victorious in 1945 led many Americans to overestimate our long run virtue and strength, leading the frustration and disappointment, particularly in Asia.

BOXES

BOX p. 615 "Winston Churchill's Leadership" [written record]. These famous speeches are not only a "written record" but one preserved in audio recordings as well.

BOX p. 624 "The Final Solution" [written record]. There are fifty volumes of testimony and documentation from the major Nuremberg trial, much of it as vivid as this one. It is all available on a single compact disk. You may wish to use clips from the film "Schindler's List" or one of the many excellent documentaries in class.

BOX p. 635 "Soviet-American Rivalry and the Cold War" [closer look]. This excerpt from Kennan's well known article is an addition to this edition of the textbook. We can observe it now with post-cold war eyes.

BOX p. 638 "America's Stake in Vietnam" [written record]. This early speech by Kennedy (1956) shows how the United States got involved in that country. Some forty years after this statement, and twenty years after our loss of that war, we can judge the accuracy of his statement.

Now let us turn to the specific subheadings of the chapter for consideration of important details.

I. INTERNATIONAL POLITICS BETWEEN THE WARS

Though the Treaty of Versailles had many flaws, and though it did not set the stage for a century a relative stability as had the Congress of Vienna a century earlier, one could argue that it was not so bad that it necessarily <u>caused</u> World War II. Indeed, at the Locarno meetings, and with the Dawes and Young plans mentioned earlier, the worst aspects of the Treaty seemed their way to being repaired.

The one aspect of the World War I settlements which still seemed out of control was the isolation of the Soviet Union. Lenin, Stalin, and the other Soviet leaders brought this on themselves, to some extent, by their attempts to further the cause of "World Revolution." Try to get the students to "check their guns at the door" and see things from the Soviet angle at first. Then you can return to a critique of Soviet policy during the Stalinist period.

TO DEFINE AND DISCUSS

"twenty years' truce" in Europe
Washington Naval Conference
Treaty of Rapallo
Zinoviev letter
Litvinov

II. THE ROAD TO WAR

Note how the "steps" shift back and forth amongst the continents, with 5 of the 8 being in Europe, 2 in Asia, and 1 in Africa. This is a useful analysis and emphasizes the world-wide nature of the brewing conflict. But students should be made aware that these particular "8 steps" are put together by the textbook authors, and other analysts may see things a bit differently.

The concept of *appeasement* is very important. During the 1930s, many men and women thought of appeasement as a wise policy of avoiding conflict by recognizing the vital interests of major powers rather than seeking conflict. It was seen by its advocates, therefore, as a means of conflict resolution. The failure of appeasement led the United States, after the war, to take a very tough "containment" line vs. any new potential aggressor, and the historical justification was called upon again in 1990 to explain the Gulf War.

TO DEFINE, LOCATE, AND DISCUSS

German rearmament and remilitarization of the Rhineland
the Italians at Adowa and again in Ethiopia
Franco and the Spanish Civil War
the "Rome-Berlin Axis"
Japanese attacks on China 1931 and 1937
Sudeten Germans and the Czech crisis
the Polish corridor and Danzig

III. WORLD WAR II, 1939-1942
&
IV. VICTORY FOR THE UNITED NATIONS

World War II began as a war of motion, partly because of the new technology and partly because of the ruthlessness of the aggressors. The German successes in Europe caught the Allies by surprise and demoralized them. But Britain could not be attacked directly, and Hitler turned his guns to the East to achieve his long run goal of *Lebensraum*. Like Napoleon, Hitler was stopped as much by the weather as by the battles. Stalingrad in the East and El Alamein in North Africa marked the turning points against the Soviets and Anglo-Americans respectively. D-Day was important, but it did not determine the outcome of the war, because by 1944 Hitler was being defeated in any case.

The Japanese attack on Pearl Harbor was a risky attempt to cripple the United States fleet. It enraged the United States and the tide was turned in the Pacific War the following year at Midway. The atomic bomb brought a quick end to the war, which ultimately the Japanese would have lost in any case.

TO DEFINE, LOCATE, AND DISCUSS

Maginot line
Luftwaffe
the Winter War with Finland
Dunkirk
Vichy France
Hirohito
Rommel
Sicily
Battle of the Bulge
Tito
the "final solution"
Iwo Jima
Yalta Conference of the Big Three
"unconditional surrender"

V. THE COLD WAR BEGINS
&
VI. CONFLICT IN ASIA

Some may argue that United States involvement in Europe after 1945 and its part in the two wars on the edges of the Asian mainland, Korea and Vietnam, are two very different things. But to Americans they were all part of a long term effort to avoid the appeasement of Communism throughout the world. World War II left two great powers, the United States and the USSR, each with its own ideology, its own bloc, and ultimately with its own stockpile of nuclear weapons. The United States took its new role as leader of the "free world" very seriously, and the long war in Vietnam escalated to unanticipated proportions. In Europe the blocs stabilized along what Churchill called the Iron Curtain until the collapse of the communist empire 1989/1990.

Were these wars, hot and cold, all fought to keep the world safe for democracy against a centralized Communist threat? So it seemed until the Soviet-China split showed that the "reds" were not as centrally directed as many thought. Where will these confrontations arise again? Africa? Latin America? The Middle East?

With the end of the Cold War, what does the new world order look like? Is the thermonuclear threat now gone, or has it assumed new and more unpredictable forms, now that many more countries have the potential for atomic weapons?

SUMMATION

In terms of chronology, it makes some sense to see the entire period of 1931-1989 as a massive struggle for power, in which the United States finally emerges with hegemonic power. Yet, the complexities of the period would surely be done great harm if we were to forget the various parts of the struggle in an attempt to subsume it all in a single concept. Students look at World War II as the war against Hitler and his ilk, and perhaps that makes sense after all. Still, the cold war is more than merely "aftermath," as the next two chapters will make very clear.

CRITICAL THINKING

Students who like discussing current affairs may have trouble putting the present day in perspective. But you should help them ask the right questions about the events of their parents' generation so they can make history work for them. In what respects were the two great wars of the twentieth century like the Napoleonic wars of the early nineteenth? What effects did democratization have? Are we talking about another Hundred Years' War here, or another Thirty Years' War? Does it make any sense to look for historical precedents when one is faced with the ultimate threat of atomic warfare? What will foreign relations be like when your youngest student is at the age of retirement?

27. TWENTIETH-CENTURY THOUGHT AND LETTERS

The MAJOR GOAL of this chapter is to familiarize the students with the intellectual trends of the past eight decades or so, and to raise questions in their minds about the nature of history as a discipline. The previous chapters on the twentieth century have pretty systematically left out the history of ideas and the arts, unlike the earlier chapters, so here is the chance to make up some time. Unfortunately, you may be running out of time at the end of the term (or your students will be), so this chapter may not get the attention it deserves.

Here is a suggestion. Assign this chapter--or at least the first section of it--at the very beginning of the course. It gives a good introduction to the discipline of history and to the views of the author(s).

The NINTH EDITION closely follows the Eighth Edition. However, it should be noted that the eighth edition differs markedly from the seventh and earlier editions. In 1992 this chapter was renumbered (in the Seventh Edition it was Chapter 28, the final chapter) and extensively rewritten. If you have been using the earlier edition, you might do well to begin by comparing closely the summary sections of the two chapters. Generally, this chapter has been informed by the perspectives of growing environmentalism and the collapse of communism in eastern Europe. The term "postmodern," which was cautiously introduced in Chapter 22 and might have been expected to be emphasized in this chapter, has been avoided.

BASIC OBJECTIVES

1. The students should be able to demonstrate a basic understanding of the following terms used in the subsection titles.

modernity
historicism
elite vs. popular

2. The student should recognize and be able to identify and/or define the following major items from the chapter.

artifact
archaeologist
Sigmund Freud
behaviorism
existentialism
seminology
Spengler's *Decline of the West*

Albert Einstein
green-house effect
William Faulkner
James Joyce
Picasso
Henry Moore
the Beatles

3. Students should appreciate the social "sciences," which have been part of Western intellectual life since the Enlightenment, but have developed as academic disciplines and have gained political and social power in the twentieth century. Some historians lament that they have virtually crowded "true" history out of the academy, whereas others appreciate what they have done to broaden the definition of history.

4. A great many students will think of history as little more than "past politics." Whether you use this chapter at the beginning or at the end of your course, be sure to reenforce the idea that history is a great deal broader than that. All truly devoted historians, of course, will argue that it is actually the Queen of the Sciences, bringing together all knowledge in the supremely integrative discipline. (Skeptics will call it the "jack of all trades and the master of none.")

5. Writing about contemporary culture is a difficult thing for an historian (indeed many historians argue that it is impossible and decline to try). After reviewing this chapter, what do you think of the authors' efforts? What would you have put into the chapter or deleted from it?

QUESTIONS FOR DISCUSSION

1. What does the word _modern_ mean? Or, to phrase it more precisely, how is the word _modern_ use by historians?

Note the traditional divisions of _ancient_, _medieval_, and _modern_, by which definition all of Volume II of this book will deal with "modern." However both academic and popular usage can vary. Derivations like _pre_modern, _post_modern, and _modernization_ demonstrate the importance of this concept to the historian.

2. Compare and contrast the developments in the sciences during the twentieth century with the developments in the arts, both popular and elite. Are we living in an age of reason, or of unreason?

Note the complexity of Einstein's and Freud's world, as compared to Newton's and Locke's. The relate that to the non-representational art and the modern novelists, poets, and musical composers. Is pop culture a reversion to something direct and understandable, or just a more earthy version of the newest of elite culture?

3. Describe and critique the philosophies of history which are grouped under the rubric of "historicism."

Note that historians and philosophers are often after the same basic and cosmic understandings. Marx had his all-encompassing view of history. Spengler and Toynbee each contributed their own view of where history was going. Each can be critiqued by comparing their theories with the realities described in the course as a whole.

4. Compare and contrast the vision of one "Western" civilization with that of a world culture. How has the twentieth century brought these competing concepts toward a convergence?

Note the obvious convergencies of time and space, with jet planes, computers, microwave dishes, etc. But note also the more subtle aspects of convergence as the world modernizes. Women and men all over the globe work in factories or offices, read a national and international press (if they read at all), and watch television and sports for entertainment. Pop music and Coke are ubiquitous, East and West, North and South. With the end of communist totalitarianism in central and eastern Europe, the similarities are even more clear.

BOXES

BOX p. 645 "The Age of the Computer" [doing history]. Note that this passage is dated 1974. Twenty years ago even high-powered research computers often had less power than the PC on which I write this manual. Ask your students, many of whom will be used to the latest thing in computers (or at least in computer games) whether the passage still rings true.

BOX p. 647 "Freud on Modern Civilization" [written record]. Freud's insights into humankind and its personal and social problems continue to inform the twentieth century. Perhaps his ideas will be the enduring legacy, long after the idols of pop culture are replaced by ones new and improved. What would your students think?

BOX p. 655 "Faulkner on Human Security" [written record]. "When will I be blown up?" In the post-cold war age, is that still the grave anxiety of our age? Poll your students, and see what they think. Have them evaluate this document within the context of its time (1949), just as they would do with Pigafetta's description of sixteenth-century voyaging (p. 293).

Now let us turn to the specific subheadings of the chapter for consideration of several important details.

I. THE MODERNITY OF HISTORY
&
II. MODERN THOUGHT ABOUT HUMAN NATURE

The study, teaching, and learning of history, both formally and informally, is still a major activity, no matter how professional historians lament the decline of the discipline in the popular mind. Historical loves and hates, hopes and fears, lie at the base of many political and cultural issues of our time. In the 1980s court cases in the United States asserted that history had been perverted by the cutting of nearly all mention of religion in our books and classrooms. Other groups have lobbied to put the history of their particular group into the books, with only favorable mention, to be sure. Particular ethnic groups maintain that their own group should stand at the center of all history. In the 1990s the Congress has debated the appropriateness of curricular guidelines for United States and World History. History is likely to remain controversial for a long time to come. If it is any good, it *should* be controversial.

The social sciences and the humanities in our age seem caught in the dilemma of trying to solve the broadest of problems, but trying to do so by emulating the research of the natural sciences. Thus professional historians and the -ologists seem to be telling us more and more about less and less. Those of us who take seriously the charge to teach introductory courses in modern civilization, and our students who try to keep up with the material, are left with a daunting task.

TO DEFINE AND DISCUSS

the "moment of modernity"
secular humanity
the *id*, *ego*, and *superego*
Pareto, Sartre and "existence is prior to essence"
cyclical rise and fall
consensus history

III. TWENTIETH-CENTURY SCIENCE

Students in introductory science classes, despite the best efforts of the best of their instructors, will probably come away with the idea that science is made up of endless pages of true facts and immutable laws. This chapter should give you the chance to upset that idea by emphasizing the provisional nature of scientific knowledge. The term <u>relativity</u> has given rise to a great deal of misunderstanding about modern science, to be sure, but it can be used to remind students that Newtonian physics--once thought to be immutably true--has been replaced (for many purposes) by Einstein's physics.

TO DEFINE AND DISCUSS

$E=mc^2$
the *quantum*
the *quark*
the indeterminacy principle
biological warfare
the green revolution in agricultural production
Max Planck
George Perkins Marsh

IV. MODERN LITERATURE AND THE ARTS: ELITE AND POPULAR

Outside of the academy does anyone read the great novelists and poets, perform or hear the works of serious musical composers, or pause to appreciate the latest in painting or sculpture? As a matter of fact they do. In spite of the apparent dominance of commercial mass pop culture, more people are involved in the elite culture of our civilization than ever before. By the same token, popular culture is being seriously studied within the academy as a key to understanding the social history of our age.

Students may argue with you that _modern_ music is Bruce Springsteen, "Pearl Jam," or whoever might be at the top of the charts on a given week, while ignoring the modern orchestral composers like Philip Glass. I would suggest that the Springsteens of today's culture are akin to the town pipers who appeared in Breughel's paintings, i.e. they are basic recreational music for the common people. The difference is that they reach star status because of modern mass communications and marketing. Both elite and popular culture have their place in any society, but they tend to overlap in our democratic world.

TO DEFINE AND DISCUSS

T. S. Eliot
Mickey Mouse
Agatha Cristie
Surrealism
Frank Lloyd Wright
Elvis
the Sony Walkman
John Lennon

SUMMATION

History is supposed to bring perspective, and it is fitting to return to some recurring questions which have haunted our civilization and which continue to do so? What it the good, the true, and the beautiful? How does an individual--and a society--discover these things, nurture and protect them, and pass them on to future generations? What is the relationship between freedom and equality, between the rights of the individual and the rights of the group? How can we keep the world from ending, either with a bang or a whimper?

CRITICAL THINKING

Try convening your class as if they were living 100 years into the future, and ask them to look back at the thought and letters of the twentieth century. Have them try to decide which creative artists will still be remembered, and for what. Use the pictures in this chapter, and the BOXES as examples to get them going.

28. OUR TIMES: ARRIVING AT THE PRESENT

The MAJOR GOAL of this chapter is to familiarize the students with the post-1945 world, starting with Western Europe and North America and going virtually around the world. In a sense it is a briefing on current affairs, though more long term historical understandings are not ignored. If some of the rest of this book can be criticized for bypassing the non-western world, this chapter most certainly cannot.

The NINTH EDITION is based directly on the Eighth Edition, in which this chapter, originally numbered 27, had been moved to number 28. There have been major additions, particularly dealing with China and the Middle East. All sections have been updated through 1994. The BOXES have been thoroughly revised. The chapter, and the book, ends with a thoughtful section called "perspectives."

BASIC OBJECTIVES

1. There are no new terms in the chapter subheadings this time for students to learn, but there are geographical names. You might be surprised at how little basic geography your students know, even after they have had your course up till this point. Try handing out a plain outline map of the world and ask them to shade in the following areas: Great Britain, Germany, India, Pakistan, and Canada. If they do not do well . . .

2. The students should be able to recognize, identify, describe, or locate all of the following items.

AIDS
European [Economic] Community (Common Market)
decolonization
apartheid
Rhodesia/Zimbabwe
Fourth and Fifth Republics
NATO and Warsaw Pact
Konrad Adenauer
Nuremberg Trials
Khrushchev
Solzhenitsyn
Gorbachev
West Pakistan
East Pakistan/Bangladesh
Indira and Rajiv Gandhi
OPEC
Israel
Nasser and Sadat

Saddam Hussein
Palestine and PLO
Iran/Iraq War
Nkrumah
Qaddafi
Nigeria and Biafra
Cuba
Sandinista
Rabin and Arafat

3. This chapter is worldwide, but centered on the United States. That is to say, it is organized to give Americans information so that they can understand the world news. If you have TV tape capability you might bring in a few segments of the evening news, freezing frames to give your students an oral quiz on what is going on, and where.

4. Students should know that some historians once believed that European domination of the world was destroyed forever by World War II. This chapter shows both the truth and the limitations of that statement. Europe recovered--the West quickly, the East less quickly--and has more economic power and prosperity than ever before. Yet Europe no longer controls the world. Power migrated to the superpowers of the United States and the USSR during the Cold War, but even they were limited in what they could do to impose their wills on other lands, as both Vietnam and Afghanistan showed. Now the United States has achieved a kind of hegemony in terms of world power, while the countries of the former USSR are taking their places among the secondary powers and the client states (and sometimes unruly ones at that) of the world.

5. The additions to this chapter are significant, but the basic structure of the chapter is virtually unchanged. It might be interesting to speculate, with your students, how the history of the 1980s and early 1990s might look to historians writing in the year 2000 or even 2095.

QUESTIONS FOR DISCUSSION

1. Marx, Engels, and Lenin all argued that capitalism would fall as the workers of the world rose up and cast off their chains. Where and by what means did Marxism grow since between 1945 and 1970? Where and by what means did it lose power in the 1980s and 1990s?

Note both the geographic spread of communism and the variety of its forms. In no place did a Marxist government come to power in a highly developed bourgeois capitalist industrialized society as Marx predicted. Soviet bayonets in Eastern Europe and peasant revolutionaries elsewhere created the new communist states. Note the abiding significance of nationalism and individualist capitalism in undermining communist states.

2. Considering the period 1945-1970, compare and contrast the states of the Western bloc and the Eastern bloc in Europe, with regard to their political systems, economic progress, and international arrangements.

What factors after 1970 made the states more similar, until by 1990 the "blocs" no longer had their former meaning?

Note that both NATO and the Warsaw Pact were, in their own ways, successful. But an Iron Curtain divided them until 1989, symbolized by the Berlin Wall.

3. What was the relationship between the Cold War and the end of the old colonial empires?

Note that the anti-colonial fighters, like Ho in Vietnam, found ready allies in the Marxist-Leninist states. On the other hand, the United States found itself apparently propping up former colonial collaborators, in the name of the "free world." The reality of Soviet neo-colonialism was seen clearly, however, in Afghanistan.

4. Could the American Revolution serve as a more attractive model for the anti-colonialists of the Third World than the Bolshevik revolution?

Note the eighteenth-century context of the American Revolution and the twentieth-century context of the Bolsheviks. Nevertheless, "life, liberty, and the pursuit of happiness" remain attractive today, and the excesses of the Marxists-Leninists--especially Stalin and Mao--have been rejected even by the new leaders in Moscow and Beijing.

5. Consider the "prospects" at the end of this chapter. What genuine progress has occurred in our history, and why does the author appear optimistic about the long term significance of Western civilization and its contributions to the world? Do you agree?

BOXES

BOX p. 663 "Is There a Grand Design in History?" [doing history]. these two extracts from British historians have been moved from Chapter 27. The make a fitting terminus for the series "doing history." You might review all the "doing history" items in order to see if they would give you a balanced view of what you learned "doing history" was when you were in graduate school.

NOT A BOX p. 670, but serving a similar purpose, are the gathered photographs of twelve women who have led their countries over the past few years. Missing is Mrs. Thatcher, because she was only the "head of government" rather than head of state. No Americans made the page.

BOX p. 673 "I Have a Dream" [written record]. Martin Luther King's magnificent speech deserves reviewing in the context of world history. Note that he is always called "<u>Martin Luther</u> King," not just Martin King, and there is a reason for that which you might discuss with your students. His dream is based on the Enlightenment ideals of "inalienable rights" for all men (and, no doubt, for all women).

BOX p. 675 "Let the Word Go Forth" [written record]. Kennedy combines the toughness of a cold warrior who sent troops to Vietnam with the idealism of the president who gave us the Peace Corps.

Now let us turn to the specific subheadings of the chapter for consideration of several important details.

I. WESTERN EUROPE
&
II. NORTH AMERICA

There was a huge rebuilding job to do in Europe after the war, much greater than that after World War I. The Marshall Plan involved the United States from the first, not just with relief supplies but with investment. And, more uniquely, not just with former allies but also with former enemies. This is a remarkable contrast to the reaction of the United States after World War I. We should not assume a "holier than thou" attitude about this initiative, however, because there was shrewd self-interest involved.

The parallel, but different, growth patterns of the states of the Western bloc bear some watching. Is the USA likely to find itself going the way of Great Britain, losing its position of industrial leadership? The BOX on relative British decline has been deleted in this edition, but the question still is worth asking.

TO DEFINE AND DISCUSS

Attlee and Harold Wilson
Volkswagens
race riots in England
Irish Republican Army
the Algerian war
"Europe of Fatherlands"
Mitterand
"guest workers"
Willy Brandt
Helmut Kohl
Christian Democrats
terrorism
Vatican II Council
John Paul II
post-Franco Spain
Scandinavian monarchies and socialism
Eisenhower
McCarthism
racial integration
the Kennedys
Nixon, China, and Watergate
Ronald Reagan and Thomas Jefferson
French and English in Canada
Panama
Latin American immigrants to the USA

III. THE EASTERN BLOC

Stalin's USSR survived the Second World War, and those who hoped that liberalization would follow in the wake of peace were disappointed. After Stalin's death some liberalization did occur, and the developments were hesitant and inconsistent. Alternate thawing and freezing is interesting to watch for the historian, but it very tough on road to the future.

This section has significant material on *glasnost* and *perestroika*, mentioning Boris Yeltsin and Lech Walesa as well as Gorbachev.

When I wrote the manual for the Seventh Edition, in 1987, Gorbachev was just celebrating the seventieth anniversary of the Great Socialist Revolution by announcing that historians would be free to study and write about the sins of the Stalinist past. I expressed myself skeptically about the immediate future: "Attempts to liberalize communist states began with high hopes in Hungary during the 1950s, Czechoslovakia in the 1960s, and Poland in the 1970s, but revolutionary discipline always had to reimposed. Consider Cromwell in the seventeenth century and the Jacobins in the eighteenth. Perhaps enough time will have passed now to prove Craine Brinton right (or wrong) after all."

In fact, historians in the USSR and its successor states had tremendous freedom over the past years, and political and economic freedoms have expanded as well. Yet the whole procedure has proven to be somewhat destabilizing. You may wish to discuss comparative revolutions with your students: a good way to let them know that they are much more sophisticated consumers of political news now that they have had your course and read this book.

TO DEFINE AND DISCUSS

Soviet space accomplishments
Pasternak and Yevtuschenko
Afghanistan
Chernobyl
glasnost and *perestroika*
German reunification

IV. THE NON-WESTERN WORLD IN INTERNATIONAL AFFAIRS

If Westerners did not realize it in 1905, the Japanese expansion of World War II clearly demonstrated that one did not have to be white, or European, to create modern machines and use them to demonstrate power in world affairs. After the defeat, under American tutelage but with their own skill, Japan became what Britain had once been--the workshop of the world. Other Asian nations came along as well.

The rise of the great oil cartel, which put power in the hands of a few oil-rich but otherwise underdeveloped states, introduced yet another factor into the world economy. Europe has little oil and the United States has insufficient quantities for the needs of her high living standards. Thus a new economic balance of power has emerged which has little or nothing to do with the superpower blocs which seemed to dominate the post-war world.

Moreover, each of these countries have their own nationalistic agendas to which Soviet-American relations might be irrelevant. The Arab-Israeli dispute, the Iran-Iraq war, the Cyprus question, the Falkland Islands, and a hundred others do not fit into simplistic dualistic model of "free world" vs. "Godless communism." That dualistic struggle may indeed have been very important for world history between the end of World War II and the late 1980s, and at may reemerge in some new form as we approach the year 2000. The textbook appears a bit cautious about declaring the cold war over once and for all. I suppose if the amazing changes over the past several years teach us anything it is to be cautious about making pronouncements. An American historian I know who lives in Berlin told me that after the sudden fall of the Berlin wall he had gotten out of the prediction business once and for all.

TO DEFINE AND DISCUSS

nationalism in former colonies
Greater East Asia Co-Prosperity Sphere
Nixon in China
Tiananmen Square
Syngman Rhee
Sukarno and Suharto in Indonesia
Marcos and Aquino in the Philippines
Hindi vs. English in India
the 1956 Suez crisis
terrorism and freedom fighters
kibbutz
My Lai massacre
Jomo Kenyatta and the Mau Mau
F. W. de Klerk and Nelson Mandela
Chile and the CIA
the Peróns and Argentina
the Cuban revolution
Grenada
Panama
Kuwait

V. PROSPECTS

There is much discussion in the academy today about whether it is necessary or appropriate to emphasize "Western" culture. I suppose if you or your institution had not already made a decision to take the "Western" approach, you would not even be using the Winks, Brinton, Christopher and Wolff textbook or reading this manual. But it may still be useful to raise this question of appropriateness with your students for discussion and reflection. This final section provides a carefully considered justification for recognizing the importance of Western civilization for special study, though it never claims that other civilizations are lacking in worth or significance. The importance of

Western civilization goes beyond politics and elite culture, to the emancipation of women, the importance of science and technology, and the fact that the breadth of vision of our civilization has (at its best) opened its promises to the entire world.

SUMMATION

A history of civilization is less a set of facts than a set of questions. To give thoughtful and worthwhile answers, of course, substantial knowledge is necessary. But mere lists of names and dates are in themselves no more important than lists of telephone numbers. Perhaps nowhere is that more clear than in a chapter in which authors try to look at their own times with the tools of the historian. Careful weighing of evidence, analysis of trends, and efforts to maintain unbiased judgment, are all terribly necessary for understanding contemporary events. But the two elements which historians especially treasure about their craft, the ability to get into the private records of the participants--rather than simply taking their public pronouncements--and the perspective which comes with time, and are inevitably missing.

Yet what is one to do? If we abandon contemporary history to publicists, politicians, and social "scientists," we--as historians and history teachers--have lost the opportunity to make an immediate impact upon the world in which we live, and we may have lost much of our audience as well.

CRITICAL THINKING

One way to test whether your course has been successful for you and your students is to bring into class this week's edition of *Time*, *Newsweek*, the *New York Times*, *Der Spiegel*, *L'Express*, or any other major news source you have handy, and go through it cover to cover with your students. A good history of civilization should prepare one to understand and critique that news source, or at least to appreciate everything that has gone into its pages.

SUGGESTED READINGS

At the end of the textbook is a list of books designed to be very useful for you and for your students. It is not a bibliography of works consulted during the writing of the textbook. Instead, it is a selection of books appropriate for undergraduate readers who want to find out more about a particular subject. Each entry also contains a brief and helpful notation, so one has some idea about what the book is like.

The list is organized in the same format as the chapters themselves, so it is relatively easy to look up a book by subject. But each section is separated from the chapter to which it refers, so most students will never even look at it unless you teach them to do so. Here are several suggestions.

1. At the beginning of the course go through the book quickly with your students, cover to cover, initiating discussion (or at least recitation) about each section of the book. This way they will see what they (or someone else) has spent so much money to acquire for their use. (You can also use this opportunity to point out the virtues of the INDEX, one of which is that pronunciations are given for unfamiliar words.)

2. When you are in the midst of a given subject, instruct the students to check to see where they might find out more details. Their initial reaction will be to go to their library's catalogue, but they will soon learn to go to the SUGGESTED READINGS first.

3. I have a bias in favor of reading history books which are not textbooks. If you are using this textbook you have already made a major commitment of resources (time and money) for a lengthy textbook, so your students will probably not be able to do a number of "outside readings." But they may be able to do one or two. Having them select from this list is a good idea, because Robin Winks has chosen books most of which are relatively short, at the reading level of beginning undergraduates, and many of which are currently available in paperback.

4. Few of us are totally happy with the library holdings of our institutions. If you need a relatively up to date list of good history books for your undergraduate library, here it is. You might find someone to check your holdings against this list and then request purchase of the items which you do not have.

AFTERWORD

In Europe those who teach history, and those who write the books with which one teaches history, like to speak of "history didactics." In fact there is an "International Society for History Didactics" with its headquarters in Germany. The term sounds terrible in English, because the world "didactic" has the ring of something that is overblown, preachy, and condescending. But what these scholars and practitioners mean by the term is the serious consideration of what one learns from history and how one learns it. Every time you go into a classroom, every time you draft a lecture, prepare a syllabus, write a test, or write material for your students or for other teachers, you are engaging in the craft of history didactics. Beyond the academy history didactics comes in to play as well, in the mass media, in public celebrations, and in popular culture.

There's an old conundrum which asks whether, if a tree falls in the forest and no one is there to hear it, would it make a noise? It might be paraphrased as follows: if an historian does research but never writes or teaches about it in a way that it can be understood, does it make an impact? I guess that paraphrase suggests the significance of history didactics, and of what we do as historians and as teachers. We want to make sure that the historical crashes to the forest floor do not go unheard.